Great story of a turnaround of a company using the TWI JI, JR, JM and Kata methodologies. Very enjoyable read with ideas that can be implemented quickly in any company.

Paul D. Hill
Manager of Continuous Improvement, Cosma Canada US;
A Division of Magna International

In a heart warming, easy-to-read story Alley has made the concepts of TWI (Training Within Industry) easy to understand and more importantly gives you a sense of how transformational TWI can be. Whether you are a first line supervisor or general manager, experienced or brand new, this book gives you the tools and practices to be better at your job.

Ben Hume
Former National Chair,
Canadian Manufacturers & Exporters

The questions for reflection at the end of each chapter will be helpful for leaders at many different levels, whether new or experienced. The supervisory tools introduced in the book are practical and effective.

Jason Waters
Manager, Western Canada Parts Distribution Centre,
Toyota Canada

A great read, a great story, great lessons, and powerful learning for new and experienced supervisors. I couldn't wait to see how it ended!

Anne C. Graham
#1 Best Selling Author – Profit in Plain Sight

Becoming the Supervisor

Becoming the Supervisor
Achieving Your Company's Mission and Building Your Team

Hugh R. Alley

A PRODUCTIVITY PRESS BOOK

First published 2020
by Routledge
52 Vanderbilt Avenue, New York, NY 10017

and by Routledge
2 Park Square, Milton Park, Abingdon, Oxon, OX14 4RN

Routledge is an imprint of the Taylor & Francis Group, an informa business

© 2020 Hugh R. Alley

Library of Congress Cataloging-in-Publication Data

Names: Alley, Hugh R., author.
Title: Becoming the supervisor : achieving your company's mission and
building your team / Hugh R. Alley.
1 Edition. | New York : Routledge, 2020. | Includes
Identifiers: LCCN 2020002448 (print) | LCCN 2020002449 (ebook) | ISBN
9780367862190 (paperback) | ISBN 9780367893262 (hardback) | ISBN
9781003018575 (ebook)
Subjects: LCSH: Leadership. | Problem solving, | Decision making. | Teams
in the workplace--Management. | Organizational effectiveness.
Classification: LCC HD57.7 .A4225 2020 (print) | LCC HD57.7 (ebook) | DDC
658.4/022--dc23
LC record available at https://lccn.loc.gov/2020002448
LC ebook record available at https://lccn.loc.gov/2020002449

ISBN: 978-0-367-89326-2 (hbk)
ISBN: 978-0-367-86219-0 (pbk)
ISBN: 978-1-003-01857-5 (ebk)

Typeset in Garamond
by Lumina Datamatics Limited

This book is for

Alicia, André, and Derick, and all the other leads and supervisors who taught me so much and showed me how much difference these skills can make;

and for

Rebecca and Ted, my children, and for children everywhere, with the hope that they will always have meaningful work that they love and great bosses;

and for

Diana, without whom I would accomplish very little, and who always calls me to be my best.

Contents

List of Figures

List of Tables

Preface

In song and story, it is widely recognized that most people are happy to work for their pay. They're not after a handout. This is what I see in the workplace. People are willing to work, especially when they go home at the end of their shift thinking they have done something worthwhile, something that will make a difference. We humans like to think we've made a contribution.

Dorothee Sölle, the noted Christian theologian, argued that humans are made for two things: love and work. She argues that our society's aversion to work has more to do with the soul-less tedium that most people experience when they labour for wages than it does with any fundamental unwillingness to work. And when I challenge supervisors, they grudgingly admit that most people don't start their day with the idea of making someone else's work life miserable.

Yet it seems that this desire to work is not the stuff of popular experience. Articles regularly report how frustrated people are by their workplace. Polls repeatedly tell of large numbers of individuals disengaged from their work. We see it in the surprise so often expressed when someone talks about work they love. And the widespread nature of the malaise is shown in the chatter of radio hosts who harp on the theme that it is only so many days until the weekend (when, presumably, we come to life again).

As supervisors and managers, we play a big role in people's experience of work. Regardless of what is going on in the company, how your boss treats you matters. If you are a boss, how you treat those who work under your direction matters. As one of my mentors puts it, if we as bosses treat people like human beings, they're less likely to go home and kick the cat – or anyone else. More than one survey has reported that the number one reason people leave a workplace is being badly treated by their boss.

I've seen the damage a bad boss can do. Early in my career I worked in a company where the absence of skill among the managers and supervisors was a major contributor to a toxic culture. The extent of the problem was highlighted when the new HR manager came in to the president and me one evening with the advice that we should "shut it down." We looked at him somewhat stunned, because we both knew him as an unfailingly positive person. "This company is making people into worse people," he observed. The impact of that comment has never left me. As you might imagine, not much later the company went under.

Twenty years later I stepped into another company with the signs and smells of similar toxic culture. I needed to fix it, and fast. At its core, the skills of the supervisors and team leads needed to improve dramatically. After some false starts, we landed on the idea of using the Training Within Industry (TWI) model for developing front-line leaders. Starting with Job Relations, we built skills and set standards for the behaviour of our leaders. A few wouldn't or couldn't adjust and left. But most revelled in their new abilities.

The results over 3½ years were remarkable. The accident rate went down 95 percent. Measured productivity went up 10 percent a year. The capacity of our constraint operation went up 45 percent. Lead time for our core make-to-order product line went from 8.25 days to 6.25 days. Our space needs went down by almost 50 percent. These were all tangible, measurable results. But the telling changes were more subtle. We started having people come back to the plant because they'd heard about the change in the culture, and we knew they were taking less money to make the change. As importantly, we went from having virtually no suggestions from our front-line employees to seeing one to two new ideas implemented every week. Though I was the operations manager, I didn't hear about most of the improvements until they were in place because the front-line leaders knew they had authority to make changes in their area. It was exciting.

My company's experience with the power of the TWI model was not unique. The TWI program was initially developed as part of the effort in the United States during World War II to develop supervisory skills quickly and effectively. The people in the US War Manpower Commission, who were responsible for training the workforce, were facing two problems.

First, they needed skilled production workers – fast. The poster child of this problem was the lens grinder. Historically, it had taken five years to train a person to be a competent lens grinder. But officials recognized that at that rate, the war would be over before they completed the training for a single individual. Building on work from the previous 30 years, in just six months the team developed an instruction program that reduced the training time from five years to five months. The process continued to be refined, so that by 1943, one firm could take someone off the street and have them grinding high-quality lenses at full production rates in just five days.

This instruction method was then generalized to become the Job Instruction module of the TWI approach. The most stunning application was in the shipyards. In 1939, there were only 50,000 shipyard workers in the whole of the United States. They produced about a million tons of ships. By 1942 there were over 650,000 workers, a 13-fold increase, and they produced 19 million tons of ships, a 19-fold increase. That remarkable achievement was only possible because of the skills conveyed by the TWI programs, especially Job Instruction.

The second problem the War Manpower Commission faced was developing enough supervisors to oversee the work. This was a challenge, because most of the people who might have been supervisors had enlisted and were overseas. The people who were left often had only a few months more experience than the people they directed. People became supervisors in shipyards who six months before had never seen a ship! Also, women and African Americans were, for the first time, thrust into industrial supervisory roles.

To help with this, the Training Within Industry Service developed several more programs. The two core programs were Job Relations and Job Methods. Job Relations gave supervisors a way to deal with performance issues. Job Methods provided practical tools to make local improvements to the work process.

These three programs, Job Relations, Job Instruction, and Job Methods provided a sound foundation for new supervisors.

During the war years, over 2 million supervisors were trained in these methods. The results were remarkable. In a study of 600 firms that used the TWI programs, the TWI Service reported the following outcomes:

Outcome	% of Firms Reporting This Result
Reduce grievances by at least 25%	100%
Reduce time to train by at least 25%	100%
Reduce labour hours by more than 25%	88%
Increase production by at least 25%	86%
Reduce scrap by at least 25%	55%

I have seen the same impressive outcomes, both as a manager, and as a consultant. One client used Job Instruction to increase its raw quality score from 55 percent to 85 percent in just six months. Another using Job Methods achieved a 10 percent increase in production rates in just ten weeks. A third client reported that using Job Instruction, she could develop training in half the time it had taken her before, deliver it in 30 percent less time, and get better post-instruction test results.

The TWI modules are the most useful and respectful approach to developing supervisors that I've run across. They fit within the idea of a supervisor doing what they can within their own area, regardless of the surrounding corporate culture. In effect, you can do it in "stealth" mode.

Back to the plant I was running. I was convinced that the improvement in skills was central to the transformation of the company. I left the company and started a firm to share what I'd learned. Since then, I have trained almost 1,000 front-line leaders. They have many different titles: team leaders, supervisors, coordinators, managers, foremen, and so on. The common thread is that they all directed the work of others. Sometimes they had formal responsibility for the individuals; sometimes not.

The skills made a difference in the leaders' work lives, and in their personal lives, too. I lost track of how many people came back to a later session in a program to tell the group how they had used their new skills at home and the difference it had made.

I hope that the story in this book will inspire you to learn the five key skills every front-line leader needs: how to instruct, how to deal with someone not performing the way the company needs them to, how to make local improvements in the work processes in your area, how to set work priorities, and how to communicate (mostly how to listen).

The story of Trevor points at each of these skills and gives you an example of how they can play out. It is infused with the approach embedded in the Training Within Industry program, which I believe is hugely useful because it is so practical, so grounded in "how do I do that?" Your experience will inevitably be different from Trevor's. Still, I hope you find the concepts helpful and that you have fun reading the story.

Finally, my hope is that your career becomes easier because of what you learn, whether you are a front-line leader, or you manage those front-line leaders. If all goes well, your workplace will become a place where your crews can live out one part of our fundamental nature as humans; to work with joy because they can be fully human in the workplace. Then you will have fulfilled your responsibilities as a leader: to look after the mission of your organization, and to look after your people.

Acknowledgments

I couldn't have completed this book without the support of many, many people – more than I could name and I'm sure more than I even realize.

Nevertheless, there are some I need to mention. Ben Hume took a chance on me and asked me to take on the role of operations manager when I had never done anything like that job before. He did it partly on the recommendation of Rob Napoli, and I will be forever grateful for Rob's kind words. Tracy Defoe has taught me so much about how adults learn – enough that I realize I have just scratched the surface. John Willson, Anne Graham, Mike Berris, Howard Teasley, Derek Strong, the Rev. Alisdair Smith, the Rev. Linda St. Clair, the Very Rev. Peter Elliott, and others have been strong supporters of me at various points in my career, both enlarging my comfort zone and encouraging me to step out of it, particularly as I honed in on the needs of front-line supervisors.

In the last 10 years, I have taught skills to almost 1,000 front-line leaders. None of that would have happened without the interest and support of the business owners who hired me and gave me the privilege of working with their people. From their team members I learned what worked and what didn't. I heard story after story about what it was really like to oversee the front line of a business. I need to mention two in particular. Jeanette Guertin, the owner at Supreme International, in Wetaskiwin, Alberta, gave me two amazing opportunities to work with her team, and it was in working with them that I learned how powerful it is to just walk with front-line supervisors and do whatever is needed to support them. Tracy Baker, at DIRTT Environmental Solutions in Calgary Alberta, came back to me five years after I first worked with her team to tell me that the Job Relations training I did with her team was seen as the single most useful program they ever had. This was hugely encouraging.

There are, of course, people who taught me what not to do, often by their example. I learned lots from them, too, but I will leave them un-named.

The ideas in this book have come from many individuals. A few need to be mentioned. Wally Bock's concept of the two responsibilities of any leader—looking after the mission and looking after your people—has been extremely helpful. Mike Rother's work on the Toyota Kata has reshaped my idea of how to build people's abilities and has given me a conceptual framework for situating the TWI programs. Blair Singer's teaching and mentorship on facilitation, teaching and sales has shaped how I train others, and has influenced many other parts of how I think about business. The friendship and encouragement of Mark Warren, who knows so much about the Training Within Industry program, has helped me critically reflect on what I have learned from other noted thinkers in the area, especially Jim Huntzinger and Don Dinero.

The book has taken over five years to bring to fruition. Without ongoing encouragement, it would have never happened. Marissa Brinkman was my Kata coach in the last year as I experimented my way to completion. Anne Graham and Doris Bentley shared their own experiences of getting a book published and were unfailingly generous with their advice. My daughter, Rebecca, applied her fine editing skills to the manuscript and improved it. Dwayne Butcher and Jim Hunztinger at Lean Frontiers reached out to me when they heard I had a book in the works and were very supportive. Michael Sinocchi at Productivity Press helped me navigate the publishing process for the first time. And through it all, Diana, my amazing wife and partner, was the best cheerleader and encouragement I could have hoped for.

To all of you… thank you. What is good and helpful is here because of you. The shortcomings are all mine.

Author

Hugh R. Alley, PEng, is president and founder of First Line Training Inc. The company helps clients improve productivity and profits by building the skills of managers and supervisors. Hugh is an industrial engineer and has worked for over 25 years in a wide range of manufacturing settings. He has been a manager, a consultant, and a business owner. He has helped many organizations make significant gains in productivity.

Hugh has trained over 900 supervisors and front-line leaders. He has run three different manufacturing firms, including several distribution centres. He has either designed or helped with the design and fit-out of almost a dozen factories and distribution centres.

Prior to starting First Line Training in 2011, Hugh was operations manager and part owner of a manufacturing firm in Langley, B.C., with 70–120 employees. Over three years the company reduced its lead time by 25 percent, its accident rate by 95 percent, and saw measured gains in productivity of 10 to 12 percent per year. Before that he worked as part of Grant Thornton LLP's manufacturing and distribution consulting practice. He spent five years working with the Workers' Compensation Board (WCB) of BC in a range of roles including managing staff development, managing a claims unit and running several large projects. Prior to joining the WCB he spent five years running his own consulting industrial engineering firm.

Hugh has experience in a wide range of industries, including steel fabrication, pharmaceuticals, secondary wood manufacturing, mining, steel, wire, food processing, electronics assembly, appliance assembly, furniture, engineered wood products, yacht building, electrical transmission, and others. In the public sector, he has worked in education (public and post-secondary), health care, transportation, maintenance, and employment standards.

Hugh obtained his BASc at University of Waterloo (Systems Design Engineering) and earned an MSc in resource economics at Cornell, and a Master of Divinity at Vancouver School of Theology. Hugh has taught at University of British Columbia, Simon Fraser University and British Columbia Institute of Technology. He writes a regular column for *PLANT* Magazine, and he frequently writes and presents on the topics of staff development, training, lean manufacturing and quality.

Chapter 1

You Be the Supervisor

"Well, if you're so smart, why don't *you* be the supervisor?"

That's how this all started four months before. Rocky blurted it out. Now I was wondering why on earth I'd said OK.

All I'd done was make a suggestion to him about the way he'd assigned the work to our team. The way he'd done it, Sylvie was going to be waiting around for Giles to finish his work, and I suggested that I help Giles finish up his task and then go back to my work. Otherwise, I figured, we weren't going to get that order out on time.

Impulsively, I said, "Sure." I didn't have a clue what I was getting into!

Four months later, our department is slowing down the company's shipments. I'd just learned that the third important shipment this month would be late. I had a team of six people (Marcus, Steve, Zhou, and Jas, as well as Giles and Sylvie) who were waiting for me to tell them what to do to fix the situation, and I sensed that they would rather not talk to me at all. It was a far cry from four months before when I was friends with them all.

Now, Mrs. Kumar, the owner, wanted to speak with me that afternoon. I was dreading it.

Let me back up and introduce myself. Trevor Bains. I'm 28. I supervise the Raw Stock department of the Sussex Creek Boatworks, where we make a variety of wooden toy boats. We use all reclaimed wood. They're pretty high-end toys – they sell for $75–$100 each, and we ship them all over the world. I've been working here for five years.

Growing up, my dad and I made stuff in his basement workshop. I don't remember learning to use a saw or a plane, but by the time I was 11, Dad let me use the tools on my own, except the Skil saw and the radial arm saw.

We made all kinds of things: a wagon, tables, puzzles, and so on. A beautiful radio-controlled glider that we made together before he died, when I was 15, still sits on my dresser.

Learning all that from my dad, art and shop were my favourite subjects at school. I started studying business administration at college, but there was way too much sitting for my liking. I left half way through second year, without a Plan B.

A high-school buddy had landed a job at a ski resort and said they were looking for some labourers, so I went to the mountains. It was a great winter. The work was intense and physical every night once the lifts closed. We'd collapse into bed about midnight, and then we were the first ones going up the lifts in the morning. Come the summer, I hung around and got odd jobs around the resort. Then I spent another winter at the resort. I was driving one of the snow groomers, so the work was physically easier, but boy do those things throw you around a lot. Like sitting in a kitchen mixer. And they're noisy.

It was pretty easy to just slide along and do the same thing the third winter. But somewhere about March that year I realized that I didn't want to do that for the rest of my life. I finished the season and came home to visit my Mum and to think about what next.

A couple of months after I got home, Mum told me Mrs. Kumar had an opening if I was interested. The Kumars are some of our oldest friends. She and my mum became friends when I was in elementary school and they were on the Parent Advisory Committee together.

Mrs. Kumar came here as a refugee twenty-one years ago. Her son and I were in the same class. She and her husband both worked multiple jobs and went to night school to work on their English. Later I learned that she was an accountant in her home country, and he was a professor of chemistry. Four years after they arrived, they bought a small cabinet shop. They were smart, they worked hard, they made good quality products, and they were good at sales. The shop grew. Then about ten years ago Mr. Kumar got cancer and died. With Mum having lost Dad three years before, their friendship blossomed.

Mrs. Kumar carried on. Four years ago, she started up Sussex Creek Boatworks to use up the solid wood offcuts from the cabinet shop. That business took off, and now they go to cabinet shops all over the region to get enough raw material!

Not having anything else to do, I said OK. I started as a general labourer. I swept floors, emptied dust collectors, moved material through the plant, drove the company truck to collect offcuts and do deliveries, and whatever else needed doing. Rocky was the General Manager. I guess he saw that I wasn't afraid of hard work, so he kept giving me more tasks.

Then one day, about eight months after I started, when he was desperate to meet a shipping deadline, one of the saw operators called in sick. He asked me if I'd ever used wood working tools, and of course I said yes. He put me on the table saw and gave me a pile of scraps to size. I finished the lot in a couple of hours and came looking for him. He was surprised that I had already finished. After he had checked the dimensions he gave me the closest Rocky ever came to praise. "Hmmff," he said. "I guess that'll do."

That was the turning point. Over time I wound up working on all seven of the machines in the Raw Stock department. We sorted the raw offcuts by nominal size, joined them into lengths, and then converted them into rough parts for the toy boats.

Then I started working in other parts of the shop. It usually happened because Rocky was short staffed, or he had his back against the wall for some delivery deadline. After three years I'd done every job in the shop. I could even tell you who had done the previous step in the process, just by the quality of the work!

Then, as I mentioned, I made a suggestion to Rocky about how he might organize the work so we'd get an order out. He retorted, "Well if you're so smart, why don't you be the supervisor."

Without any thought, I blurted out, "Sure."

Chapter 2

The First Four Months

The day after Rocky made me supervisor things started going worse.

One of our suppliers phoned and told us that a delivery of wood we were expecting was going to be late by a day. Something about a flat tire on the delivery truck. It didn't really matter why; we were going to be out of raw material.

All of a sudden, the team was standing around asking *me* what they should do. I figured my job was to keep them busy, so I quickly came up with tasks for each person. Some cleaning. Some maintenance. But as I know now, none of it did anything to get product shipped. The team knew it, too. They poked along. At the end of the day when people went home, very little had been accomplished. Their heads hung as they slouched out of the plant.

Late that afternoon, Peter came by. He runs the assembly area. "I didn't see anything come to our area for assembly today," he said. "What's up?"

I explained the situation. "You might have let me know," he said. I could tell he was annoyed.

"Sorry," I mumbled.

"Sorry doesn't help me with my crew," he retorted, and stomped off, shaking his head.

Things were pretty chaotic the rest of that week. The Finishing department didn't have enough to keep them busy. We were late with a whole lot of shipments. And we had to do a whack of overtime to make up for the delay.

That was my first week. I didn't think I'd be supervisor very long if that happened again.

I was determined to show them I could do this, so I went up to Sally's office. She did our buying.

"Sally, can you do me a favour?"

"Sure," she said, brightly, "As long as its legal, moral, and doesn't exceed my spending limit." She grinned. Sally was always smiling. It was worth going to her office just to say "hi" to her.

"I ran out of raw material when that truck broke down at the start of this week, and we just kept tripping over ourselves trying to recover. I don't want to do that again. Could we get some of our suppliers to give us an extra supply, or speed up their next deliveries a bit, so we have some extra in stock?"

"Leave it with me," she said. "I don't see a problem. They're always asking if we want more and usually I have to hold them off. Give me a day and I'll see what I can do."

Wonderful – or so I thought. Until truck after truck arrived earlier than we expected. We had six companies that supplied most of our offcuts, and they all sent trucks a few days early. We also had another dozen companies that occasionally sent us offcuts. Within two weeks, half of them had jumped at the chance to send us an extra load.

We had so much wood that we didn't know where to put it all. We were tripping over it. Marcus, our primary forklift driver, was now spending all day moving pallets of offcuts around so we could do work.

Rocky came out to the shop to find me.

"How's the supervisor doing?" he sneered. "Got it all under control?"

"Well, it's OK, I think. I've made sure that we don't run out of wood again. That was a real problem two weeks ago. And the machines all seem to be running well. I've been getting Peter everything he needs."

"Sure," he snarled. I didn't like his tone. I've worked with Rocky a long time, and I know if you get on his bad side he can be really harsh. I'd pretty much escaped in my first five years here, but maybe that time was over.

"And I guess you think it's OK to have the shop and the yard plugged full of wood? Do you know what this has cost the company?"

"What do you mean?" I was confused. "We just pay for the wood like we always do."

"We just pay for the wood like we always do," Rocky mimicked with a sneer. "Hardly. We've spent twice as much on wood in the last two weeks as we usually do. That's drained our cash account and now we're into our line of credit, instead of having cash in the bank. We'll see how Mrs. Kumar likes that." He turned and walked away.

"Wait," I called out. But he just kept going.

Now I had two problems. Too much wood that I was having to move around all the time, and too much money spent on wood that was pushing the company into using its line of credit. I knew how much I disliked dipping into my overdraft; I could just imagine that Mrs. Kumar had the same feeling.

This supervising was getting complicated.

And so it went. Week after week I kept stumbling into more and more issues where I bumbled. My team kept coming to me for the answers, and since I thought supervisors had to have the answers, I'd come up with something.

Six weeks into the new role, Rocky asked me to come to his office. I saw Mrs. Kumar through the gap in the door. I swallowed hard, and walked in.

As soon as I was seated, Mrs. Kumar began. "Trevor, I know Rocky has given you an opportunity to be the Raw Stock supervisor. I really hope you can be successful. But the results right now are not promising. Did you know that our conversion costs for raw stock last month were 20% higher than they've been up until now? How has that happened?"

"Uh… uh…" I stammered. I didn't know! I thought back over the month. Then the light bulb went on for me. When I got all the extra wood in, Marcus had gone from spending a couple of hours a day doing forklift duties to virtually full time. To make up for his "absence" from the production side, I'd asked Peter if he had someone I could borrow. So, Ravi had come over to my department and had proved very capable. Technically, he was still one of Peter's team, but he was working for me four days out of five. I'd also noticed that the people on my team were less efficient because they were often waiting for Marcus to move a pallet for them so they could get what they needed. We'd been doing some overtime as a consequence. I hadn't really thought about it that much. But here it was in black and white. Costs up 20%.

I explained this to Mrs. Kumar. Rocky smirked. He almost seemed to enjoy watching me squirm.

"He's not as smart as he thinks, eh, Mrs. K." He smiled. "Still has something to learn. He thought he knew more than me. Phah…"

Mrs. Kumar turned to Rocky. "That's enough," she said sharply. "I don't recall you being perfect when you started here. And I expect more respect from you to your staff."

I stared at her. She had cut him off at the knees. In front of me! I didn't like where I thought this would go.

"Rocky, have you been helping Trevor learn his new role?" she asked.

"Of course," he replied. "I come over pretty often and let him know what he needs to fix."

Well that was a bit of a stretch on both counts. He came over often enough to keep the plant going, and he'd point out what was going wrong, but it sure didn't feel like I was getting any guidance. I thought the best thing for me to do was keep my mouth shut.

Mrs. Kumar continued. "Trevor, I need you to keep a steady flow of parts to the assembly area, based on our orders. If you get ahead it doesn't help us because we can't ship any faster than we can assemble, and of course we can't ship to people who haven't ordered yet." She smiled. "If you get behind, well, you've started to see the impact it has. Our customers get grumpy. They have a lot of other places they can buy cheaper toys. Or they just buy a different gift. And our costs go up, which means we get even more expensive. So too much or too little are both bad. That's your job. If you need help, speak to Rocky. He's learned a lot in his years here; sometimes he's learned the hard way." She turned and gave Rocky a wink.

"I expect you'll make some mistakes, Trevor. I'm not worried about that. But I do expect you to learn from them, and if we can all avoid making the same mistakes more than twice, we'll make out OK. I know you're sharp enough to figure this new role out." And with that, she sent me back to work and left Rocky in his office.

A couple of hours later, Rocky came by. "Not so smart are you?" he growled. "You watch yourself because I'll be watching you. I'm not going to have you mess up my production." He stalked off into the plant.

What a difference between Mrs. K and Rocky. I knew which style I liked better, but I also knew that day-to-day, I needed to make Rocky happy. And I wasn't any further ahead on how to do that.

***

The next couple of weeks were a blur. I asked Rocky where I could get cost information. He threw a couple of reports on my desk, but try as I might, I couldn't figure them out. I wasn't going to give him the satisfaction of beating me, so I started asking around to some of my friends who were also new supervisors. But they just looked at me like I was asking what kind of cheese the moon was made of. I spent several evenings in the library, but even the librarian, who'd helped me out on so many school projects, didn't understand my questions.

Meanwhile, I was fretting about how to get stuff through the plant faster. I spent time urging my team to walk a bit faster, to work a bit harder whenever it looked like we were going to be late. Sometimes I'd stay a couple of extra hours myself just to get some part ready for the next day.

All this activity didn't really make much difference. We were still struggling every day.

Then, the following week, I heard that the team was going to go to an early season baseball game on the weekend. Normally I'd have been in the thick of it, organizing everyone to have the same colour sweater or hat or something, and planning a trip to a restaurant or bar afterwards. This time, I only found out about it by accident, when I came around a corner and heard Sylvie say to Zhou as she was walking away, "See you on Saturday!"

I asked Sylvie what was up. She looked uncomfortable with my question, like she'd rather not say. "Oh, I'm getting together with a couple of the others on the weekend."

"What's going on?" I asked.

"Oh, a few of us are going to the ball game."

"Room for another?" I inquired.

"Sorry, Trevor. We could only get six tickets together and they're all spoken for. Next time...." she offered.

"Sure," I answered. But in my gut I knew there would be no next time. I suddenly realized I wasn't one of them anymore.

Before, as part of the team, I knew they had my back. I could count of them for any help I needed. Now, I was the supervisor. The Boss Man. The Whip. Anything but one of them. I didn't know if I could count on them for anything.

Over the next two months we limped along. I got more and more tired from the extra hours I was putting in. I noticed that Sylvie was late more and more often. And Marcus was just not performing as effectively as I knew he could with his forklift duties.

At least Sally had helped me with the cost information. I saw that as the piles of wood got eaten away our costs inched down – thank goodness they didn't go up.

The one thing I achieved was that I got the wood situation under control.

I'd been trying to think how I could just order when we needed some more wood. Then I thought about how my Mum always put groceries on her list on the refrigerator when she took something out of the pantry. As she explained it to me, "If I write it down when I take it from the pantry, then I know I'll have it when the kitchen supply runs out. It doesn't usually matter if I don't go shopping for a few days, because there is enough in the kitchen to last a while. So as long as I go shopping each week, I'll be fine."

I figured I could do the same sort of thing. The only trick was how to know when they took the next pallet of wood. I took a bunch of bright yellow paper, printed on it, "GIVE THIS PAPER TO TREVOR WHEN YOU MOVE THE PALLET," and taped one piece to each pallet of wood. It seemed to work. Every day or two I'd get one of the sheets, and then I'd phone Sally to get another pallet brought in.

Then three days went by with no sheets. I went out looking. I found one pallet near the jointer, half-used, and the sheet with the stretch wrap in the garbage. As I walked over to the stock area I caught a glimpse of a yellow sheet under a rack. I wondered how many others never made it to me.

Later that day I called everyone together. After some strained banter, I asked about the yellow sheets. Silence.

"Some of you must have seen these, because I've had several on my desk in the last two weeks. What's happening that I don't get them all?"

"You don't make it easy," Sylvie ventured.

"What do you mean?" I asked.

"Well, if I get one of those pallets, I'm supposed to give you the sheet, so I have to walk all the way across the plant to your office. When I do, people want to say 'hi' to me, and I'm not going to be rude, so it takes 5–10 minutes. But you're on us all the time about production. So, it's easier to just set it aside to do later. Then sometimes it slides off, or gets bundled up with the stretch wrap. I don't have time to go looking for it."

There were nods of agreement all around.

"Oh," I said, deflated. A great idea messed up by reality. How could I fix this? "OK. Thanks Sylvie. Leave it with me and I'll try to figure out a solution. In the meantime, everyone, please try to remember to give me the sheets."

I walked back to my office and called Sally. "Hey, friend, can you please arrange to bring in a couple more pallets?" I asked. "I found a couple of my sheets that got away. Not sure how I'm going to fix that," I muttered absent-mindedly.

"Will do," replied Sally. "Did you ever consider putting a tray or a clipboard on the forklift? I saw that in my cousin's factory when I visited there last year."

"Hmmm. Interesting," I answered. "And thanks."

Over the next couple of days, I thought about the problem. Sally's idea made sense. But I was sceptical. Marcus hadn't been doing a stellar job lately, and I wasn't sure he'd remember. I also didn't want to do anything that would slow him down. But at least no-one would have to walk to my office.

After three days of wondering I figured it was worth a try, so I duct-taped a tray to the back of the forklift and asked Marcus to put the sheets into the tray when he moved a pallet. He grudgingly agreed.

He came to me four hours later. "What a waste of time that is," he grumbled.

"What?" I asked.

"That tray," he replied sharply.

"What's the problem?"

"Every time I go outside the sheets blow away. I've spent 20 minutes chasing those damn sheets. Waste of my time. And you want *more* production. You'll need to do better than that."

I thought fast. What could I do? I looked around my office. There was an empty clipboard beside my desk. "Here. Try using this. It should help."

"Would have been nice if you'd thought about that before," he muttered as he turned and left.

But it worked. Every day I'd go out at the end of the day and collect the yellow sheets. And if there weren't any, I'd be able to ask Marcus about it.

To my great relief, as the amount of wood in the shop stabilized – there was a bit more than when I started, but way less than when the truckloads of wood had all shown up – our costs really did drop. Now they were only 5% more than they'd been before.

Mrs. Kumar noticed too, and said so, which was nice. But Rocky was just the same as always – hardly ever a good word.

***

The next Monday, Rocky didn't show up at all. No one knew why. Eventually, we heard that he had been rushed to hospital over the weekend. What was going on wasn't clear; I suppose it didn't matter. But it left us all in a bit of a quandary. Who would actually run the place day-to-day?

On Tuesday, I realized that there was no way we were going to get the raw material for the Central Tug order done so we could get it out on time. They were an important customer who ordered about a hundred boats a month. Some companies hand out pens and mugs. Central Tug had got in the habit of handing out our tugs. But this was the second time in four months that we were going to be late. Usually "late" wasn't too big a deal, but the shipments for Central Tug went by sea, so "late" meant we missed the ship. It would be ten days until the next ship, so unless we paid the air freight, the whole shipment would be ten days late.

Much as I dreaded it, I let Peter know that he'd only get about half the material he needed tomorrow, and the rest would be ready the day after. And that was after begging my team for some extra overtime.

Late in the day I got a short e-mail from Mrs. Kumar who wanted to see me first thing tomorrow.

With everything that had gone on over the last four months, I wasn't looking forward to it.

Reflecting on the Chapter

For Supervisors

- What was your experience when you became a supervisor?
- What is an operational problem that you faced that you have solved? What do you think helped that solution "stick"? What did your earlier experience contribute to that solution or how you implemented it?
- Have you had situations where you wish you had handled it differently? What would you have changed? What would you have needed to get the outcome you were after? New skills? Different support? Different policies?
- How has your experience as someone who has done the work helped you in your role as supervisor?

Actions to Take

- List the operational challenges you are facing now.

For Managers (you have supervisors reporting to you)

Consider all the questions for supervisors for yourself. Then consider the following.

- How many of your supervisors have been thrust into their role? How have they responded? How many of them "succeeded," as you define it? What actions have you taken that have helped them succeed?

Actions to Take

- List the operational challenges your supervisors are facing now.
- Review the training that each of your supervisors has received about how to supervise. (Distinguish between training that covered legally mandated or corporate policy-related matters and training in supervisory skills.)

Chapter 3

A New Boss

I walked into the building just before our meeting time and waited outside Mrs. Kumar's office. Exactly at 10:00 the door opened and Mrs. Kumar beckoned me in. Sitting in one of the two guest chairs was someone I hadn't seen before.

"I'm sure you've been wondering about the reason for this meeting," she began. Before I could start to reply she continued. "I want to tell you about some important news for the company." My ears perked up.

"You've probably heard that Rocky is sick. We don't know exactly what's going on, but you and I both know how important it is for someone to be with their family when they are sick, don't we?" She gave me a warm smile. Yes, we both knew that. "For the moment, the best thing for him is to be home when he isn't in hospital. I've known that he's had some health issues for several months, although he never confided in me exactly what. And Rocky is actually able to retire any time. But he loves being here, so he's just carried on. I've been very pleased for him to do so. He knows this business as well as anyone.

"However, I also have a business to run, and there are forty people whose livelihoods depend on Sussex Creek Boatworks, so I could not leave things to chance. I started looking around for a new general manager a couple of months ago. Rocky helped me because he knew that if he got much sicker, he wouldn't be around.

"I'm very pleased to introduce you to Julie Cheng, who will start here with us next week as our next general manager. Julie, please meet Trevor Bains. Trevor, this is Julie."

I stepped forward to shake her hand. I almost let my surprise show... she had a very solid handshake – much more than I'd expected from someone who was so slight.

"I'm so pleased to meet you, Trevor," Julie said. "Anna has told me how your families go back a long way together."

"They sure do," I replied. "It's a pleasure to meet you, too, Julie." I turned to Mrs. Kumar. "This isn't what I was expecting at all. And why aren't the other supervisors here, too?"

"Oh," she started, "We decided that it would be best to have each supervisor meet Julie one-on-one first. That way she can give each person her undivided attention, and have a conversation, rather than the awkwardness of meeting five people at once. That's all happening today. We'd like you to come back up here at the end of the day, and we'll have a more social time with everyone. Nothing fancy, but we've arranged for some finger food and something to drink, just to celebrate Julie joining us."

Some pleasantries followed. Then Mrs. Kumar offered, "Julie, I know you have some things you want to go over with Trevor in the next 20 minutes or so. Why don't you head over to our meeting room for that? I have some calls to make." Mrs. Kumar always had calls to make, it seems.

We walked over to the meeting room. "Mind if we stop and get a coffee?" I inquired. Normally I don't get much of a break. There is coffee available all day long, but I rarely get the chance. If I was going to be sitting down for 20 minutes, I figured I'd get while the getting was good.

"Not at all," Julie responded. "In fact, it sounds like a great idea. A fabulous idea." I was seeing the first signs of Julie's passion for coffee. Funny, but with my own limited exposure to people looking Asian, I had presumed she'd choose green tea. Such a stereotype. As I learned later, her family had been in the country for over a hundred years. She was as "local" as I was – more so actually, because my grandparents came here just sixty years ago. I guess we all make assumptions when our prejudices aren't challenged.

"So, Trevor," she began, once we sat down, "Anna tells me you just became a supervisor a few months ago. But she didn't tell me about what you did before that. Could you start by telling me about your time at Sussex Creek up until you got promoted? And congratulations, by the way. A promotion is quite a compliment coming from Anna."

Curious! I didn't realize it was that big a deal. I told Julie about how I joined the company, and how I'd done just about everything in the plant, and knew everyone pretty well except a couple of new people in the assembly area that had joined after I became supervisor. When we hire people, we like to start them there because it's actually the easiest job in the plant, and it's fun to see the boats all come together. You need more skill for finishing or to make the parts and more attention to detail in shipping.

"And how has it been for you since you became the supervisor?" she asked.

I went through the whole saga of the last four months. The wood supply issues. The performance of Marcus. The attendance issues with Sylvie. Our costs. And the latest – the late delivery for the Coastal Tug order. I figured she'd probably heard about all of these already from Mrs. Kumar.

"There's a lot on your plate," Julie commented. "A lot of problems to solve. Have you got any of them sorted out?"

I told her about the yellow sheets I was using to help me with ordering the off-cuts – our raw material. She seemed quite interested in that.

"What variations do you see in the offcuts from the different suppliers?"

"Huge variation," I laughed. "Some are really consistent in size, and they go through our system so easily. Others – you'd be hard pressed to find two pieces the same. They slow us right down. And I think the sales guys at One Tree Cabinets must really like oak because we get way more oak from them than from anyone else. There are a couple of small shops that we get a pallet from every five or six months, and when we get one of them it will all be the same species. I think they do high-end stuff, and they only work on one project at a time. It's often a weird mix of dimensions from them, too. Sometimes there will be full dimension lumber mixed in with 5 cm offcuts."

"What's the impact of that?" Julie prodded.

"It really slows us down," I replied. "We have to look at our orders and figure out which pallets to draw from, and sometimes we have a lot more work to do to create the blanks for the CNC* machine."

"I can only imagine."

"Sometimes I wish we could just focus on getting offcuts from a few companies and leave the rest. But we need the volume."

She seemed to consider this information. I waited. She started again. "What's your biggest problem right now?"

---

* Computer Numerically Controlled. This is in contrast to a manual machine where the operator controls the rate that the cutting tool moves through the material and the direction of travel. CNC refers to how the machine is controlled, rather than what it does. In this case, the CNC is actually a milling machine. In this plant, like many others, the machine is referred to by what is distinctive: in this case it was the CNC technology that was new to the plant.

"Gee. I don't know. I guess it depends on your perspective. Sylvie's attendance bugs me the most, and I'm getting lots of flack about it from the others. But I'm not sure it makes that much difference for production. Mrs. Kumar seems to ask me most about costs, but Peter seems most bothered by our department's delivery time. So, I'm not sure what's most important."

"Sounds like a lot of things going on, Trevor. I guess all that makes it hard to tell what to focus on, eh?"

"You bet. Worse than a dog in a deli."

"Well, I'm starting next Monday, and one of the things I want to do is spend some time in your area. Yours and everyone else's," she added hastily. "So, you'll probably see a fair bit of me. I'll keep my eyes open, and if I see something, I'll let you know."

"One last question before I go. Well, maybe two. Before Sussex Creek, had you ever supervised anyone?"

"Only babysitting, I guess. And I guess you could say what I did when I was a camp counsellor was supervising the kids. But for work? No."

"And when you became supervisor, what were you given in the way of training?"

"Training?" I asked incredulously. "I didn't know you could get training for being a supervisor. I sure didn't get any. Just 'You be the supervisor,' and that was it. I was on my own."

She shook her head.

"Did I say something wrong?" I asked.

"No," she said. "I'm just always amazed that so many companies wouldn't dream of bringing someone in off the street to run a half-million-dollar machine without training them. But they seem to think nothing of putting someone with no experience managing people in charge of a half a million dollars of payroll! It's nuts." There was silence for a moment. "Just so you're clear, it's not your fault," she added.

She sat back. "Well, we might as well get started on Monday." And with that, my education began.

Reflecting on the Chapter

For Supervisors

Look back on the list you made at the end of Chapter 2. Update it with any new challenges, then consider:

- What are your biggest operational challenges right now?
- Have they changed over time? What contributed to the change?
- What training, if any, have you had about how to supervise?

Actions to Take

- From your list of the biggest current operational challenges pick the *one* you think is most pressing. Consider two primary perspectives: how much it affects what your organization can deliver, and how much of your time it takes.
- Review your list and your selection with your boss.

For Managers (you have supervisors reporting to you)

Consider all the questions for supervisors from your perspective. Then consider the following.

- In your opinion, what are your supervisors' biggest challenges right now?
- What is the biggest challenge facing your boss?
- What supervisory skills would you like to develop for yourself?

Actions to Take

- Ask your supervisors what is the most pressing operational challenge they face, from their perspective. (Be careful to ask your question as an open question, rather than leading them to a specific answer. At this point, try to understand how they see the world, rather than convince them of a particular view.)

- Ask your supervisors what they are struggling with in their daily work. What is causing them worry? What concerns are they taking home with them after their shift?
- Review your supervisors' assessments of their biggest challenges and then review your own assessment. How do the two assessments match up? If the assessment is similar, reinforce it. If it is different, develop a strategy to reach a common assessment. (You may need to change your ideas!)

Chapter 4

The First Meetings

That night after dinner, I sat down at my computer and googled Julie. Who was she? I'm not sure whether I was more scared or more impressed.

She'd been educated at a really great university with a co-op program, where people alternated terms of school and work. As a result, she got her degree and two years of work experience at the same time. And had she ever worked for some amazing companies! A term with Toyota in their Toyota city complex in Japan. Two terms with a well-known technology company that is involved in space programs where she was doing testing. A term at a big US research lab. And a term with a startup company integrating robotics with prosthetic arms.

Then she'd gone to work with a company in a little town up north. They were in the middle of no-where but they were exporting their products all over the world. They were known as the best in their industry, in part because they were so innovative. She had started as a production engineer, and in the space of five years she had risen to become their operations manager. Another three years and she'd moved into sales and become their sales manager, and under her leadership they'd grown 20% per year every year. She'd been in that role for the last five years.

I found a paper she had presented at a conference that explained how they had grown productivity by 15% a year for five years in a row and had reduced their lead time from six months to six weeks.

Then I found another article that explained how the company had completely redesigned its product to cut shipping costs in half, and along the way also cut manufacturing costs by 10%.

Now, here she was at Sussex Creek Boatworks! What would bring this powerhouse to our little company? I didn't get it. Mrs. Kumar must have done some amazing sweet-talking to get her on board.

Still, I couldn't help wondering what she'd be like to work with. Those were pretty amazing results. I figured Julie would turn out to be one of those tyrants – Rocky on steroids. But that didn't make sense to me. Not with what I knew about Mrs. Kumar. I didn't think she'd put up with that style; I'd seen her cut Rocky off when he showed any disrespect. I'd wait and see.

***

Next week I came in to work same as any Monday. Traffic was unusually light so I got in about 6:30 instead of the usual 6:40. Just before 7:00 I walked through the shop; everyone was in, and they were lined up to do the work I had set for them. At 7:00 the machines started humming.

Then I went in to the office to find out what the situation was with new orders so I could work out what parts we'd need to produce this week.

Five minutes later, Julie poked her head in. "Hi, Trevor, how are you this morning?" Julie called brightly. Remembered my name, and definitely a morning person.

"Fine, thanks. How are you?"

"Great, thanks." She went on. "I'd like to meet with all the supervisors. Can you please join me at 8:00?"

"Sure, Julie." She wasn't wasting any time. "And welcome to Sussex Creek. Hope you enjoy it. It will be a lot different from that equipment company you were running." I thought I'd mention it so she'd know I'd learned a bit about her.

"Google is our friend, isn't it," she laughed. "I see you've been doing your research. Yes, it will be a change, but I expect a lot of what I learned will apply here. I find people are pretty much the same wherever I go. And thanks for the welcome. See you at 8." She walked out into the plant. She walked fast. As I learned, that was her normal speed.

I went up to speak to Sally about ordering some more off-cuts, using my yellow sheets, and caught up with her about her weekend. Then I went over to Peter's area to confirm what sequence he'd like the parts in today. I quickly approved the hours from Friday, and hurried off to the meeting with Julie.

There were eight of us in the room. Me. Peter from assembly. Sally from purchasing. Neil, our controller and payroll guy, Gil, our head shipper and logistics guy. Yvonne, our chief sales person. Farah, our product designer. And Julie of course. Arthur from the finishing department was missing.

At 8:00 am precisely, Julie started speaking. All of a sudden I was glad I'd hurried across the plant.

"As you all know, I've just joined Sussex Creek Boatworks as the general manager. I'm sorry about Rocky, and I haven't heard anything more about how he is. I'll let you know how he's doing as I hear about it. I'm really looking forward to being here and to working with you. Mrs. Kumar has spoken well about each of you, and she and I have had a lot of conversations about what I need to focus on. We'll spend more time on that in the next few weeks.

"This morning I want to tell you about how I'll be spending my time in the next month or so. It may not be what you're used to, and I don't want you to be surprised or un-nerved."

At 8:01 Arthur rushed in. He started to make apologies and Julie just held up her hand and carried on.

"You'll learn that I have some rather strongly held expectations. I'll give you this week to adjust once I've spoken to each of you. But you've already seen that being on time is one of them. Exceptions are allowed to deal with safety, accidents or imminent disaster, but my definition of disaster is pretty narrow. Late shipments and quality issues don't qualify. Organize your work accordingly.

"Now, about the next few weeks. I will be spending a lot of time where the work gets done. I'll be spending time in each of your areas. I will be going on sales calls and standing in the plant to watch what is going on. And I will want to speak to you about what I'm seeing, because I know that I'm new here, and I won't understand a lot of what I see. I want to learn, and I want you to teach me.

"I'll also be spending time with each of you to discuss your areas. Have you ever had daily meetings here?"

"Not that I can ever remember," Gil volunteered.

"I suspected as much." Julie carried on. "Tomorrow at 3 I want to meet with you all. I want to tell you about why I think a daily meeting is essential for us to improve and thrive as a team and as a company. And we can figure out what we want to have in our daily meetings.

"Any questions?"

No-one said a word.

"Well," she carried on, "I'm sure you'll have questions as time goes on. I'll do my best to answer any question you have. You may not like the answer, and that's OK. You can always ask me to explain why.

And if you think I've missed something or I've overlooked an issue, I want to hear about it. I always have time to listen, though occasionally we'll have to schedule it. Anyway, I'm going to do my best to have very open communication."

Farah cleared her throat.

"A question, Farah?" she asked.

"Well, actually, yes, if you don't mind?"

"What is it?" she inquired lightly.

"I was just wondering. I mean, you had a pretty big job at that company you were working at, eh? So I'm curious why you'd come to a tiny little company like this." She went on. Farah was like that. Once she got going... "I mean, this whole company is probably smaller than one department where you used to be!" Heads nodded around the circle. "So why would you leave a high-status job where you could probably become general manager to come to Sussex Creek. We're really small potatoes – like a pimple compared to them." Several snickers from the group.

"I heard you ask the question everyone is thinking, Farah," Julie replied. "Good question. It's actually pretty simple. My family is from here. This is where they settled when they came to this country five generations ago." Surprised looks from some of us, me included. My grandparents were the ones who immigrated. Her family had been here two generations longer than mine. "When I saw this opening, it gave me an opportunity to move back so my kids can be close to their grandparents. And I figured that by being here, I could do a bit more to help them out. You know, groceries and cleaning and stuff. And I remember how special it was to practically grow up at my grandparents' home. And then Mrs. Kumar, she agreed that I'd have a free hand to manage as I thought best."

That made some sense to me. A free hand. Near her family. And I bet that she's worked out a deal so she can earn her way into the company. That would make sense. I'm interested to see how this goes, I thought.

"Does that answer your question?" Julie looked back to Farah.

Farah nodded. "Thanks," she mumbled.

With that, the meeting dispersed.

As I walked away, Julie called out. "Trevor!" I turned to her. "I'd like to come and watch in your area tomorrow morning. Will that cause a problem?"

How could I say "no" to my new boss? "Sure," I replied. "No problem." So I'd be first.

Reflecting on the Chapter

For Supervisors

- When you started as a supervisor, what were your boss's expectations? Were they clear?
- What are your boss's current expectations? Are they clear? What is their impact on the performance of your area? Do you see those expectations as a help or as an obstacle? Why?
- What are the expectations you set for your team? Are they clear? Could your team members tell you what they are? What is their impact on the performance of your area? Of the company overall? Would they see those expectations as a help or as an obstacle? Why?

Actions to Take

- Ask two or three of your team what they think the expectations are in your company. Ask them how those expectations help them with their work, or how they hinder their work.

For Managers (you have supervisors reporting to you)

Consider all the questions for supervisors for yourself. Then consider the following.

- What are the unstated expectations in your organization that affect your area?
- What are the priorities in your organization? What always gets discussed at meetings? How does that influence your dealings with your supervisors?
- How many of the current expectations could be eliminated or altered? What would that do to the performance of your area?

Actions to Take

- Ask two or three of the people who report to you what they think the expectations are in your company. Find out which ones affect them and their work. Ask them how those expectations help them with their work or hinder their work.
- Consider what changes to the expectations might help.

Chapter 5

Her First Observations

The next morning, Julie was there when I arrived.

"Morning, Trevor. Ready for a great day?" She was almost chirping, she seemed so cheerful.

We had the usual chitchat. Then she explained that she was going to spend the next three hours standing in one place to watch what was going on.

"Doesn't that get boring?" I asked.

She explained that she learned a lot from watching. She knew that for the first hour or so she'd see lots she didn't understand, but, by the end of the three hours, she'd start to see patterns and variations to follow up on. She told me she'd never done this without learning a lot, and almost never without seeing some ideas for how to make things easier for the folks doing the work.

"OK," I agreed. "Go ahead. But shouldn't we tell them what you're doing? They're going to get pretty nervous with a new person standing there, and I don't want any accidents."

"Yes. I'm glad you think that's necessary. I was going to ask you to get everyone together for a few minutes – to introduce me, and then I can let them know what I'm up to."

I rounded up the team, turned off the exhaust blowers so we could hear, and started in. "Hi everyone." Silence. "I asked you to join me because I want to introduce you to Julie Cheng, our new general manager."

"Hi everyone," said Julie. She smiled. "It always seems a bit awkward – these first meetings with a new boss, doesn't it?" Heads nodded. "I know. I've been through enough of them. Everyone is wondering what she will say, and what's going to happen now, what different things she's going to tell us, and will it be good different or bad different?"

I was surprised that she was so direct about how people would be feeling. For all that Rocky could be a pain, we all knew what we were dealing with. Julie? Not a clue. Not yet anyway.

Julie went on. "I'm really looking forward to learning a lot from you. Mrs. K tells me that you've done a pretty amazing job of keeping up with the growth in demand. Obviously, you have lots of things about this business already figured out. I hope that I can help you make things even easier for yourselves and for our customers.

"One of the ways I learn is by watching a lot. So, this morning I'll spend about three hours just watching what is going on. I expect I'll have a ton of questions by the end of that time, and so I'll spend some time telling you what I saw, and trying to understand the obstacles that make your work harder than it needs to be.

"Does anyone have any questions?" she finished up.

There was silence for a few moments.

"I just want to know if you're going to fire us all or replace us with machines," quipped Marcus.

Julie turned to him and smiled. "Good question. I'm sorry... I don't know your name."

"She's taking names now, Marcus," smirked Jas.

"Yeah, and thanks to you, she has mine, now," he responded.

"Knock it off guys," said Sylvie. "She just got here. Show some respect."

"Thank you," Julie jumped in, turning to Sylvie. Julie obviously didn't like where this was going. "As I was saying, thank you for your question, Marcus. You're voicing a real question that lots of you must have. Let me try to answer it."

"My objective as general manager is to increase sales enough that we are both hiring *and* adding automation. I love the products this company makes. In fact, that's how I first learned about you... I bought one of your boats for my kids when my son was 2 and my daughter was 5. I bought just one to start and they fought over it," she laughed, "so I went out the next day and bought another one.

"I think there is lots of room for us to grow this business. That's behind Mrs. K hiring me. She does too. We can bring joy and fun and beauty to lots of kids and their parents. But it will only happen if we work together.

"So, to answer your question, Marcus, I expect we'll bring in automation, but not to replace people, to help us grow."

"All very well, except for the recession that's going on," Marcus responded.

"Whether there's a recession on or not, people still have birthdays and work anniversaries and get promotions and eat and live somewhere. It's been my experience that even in bad times, two out of five companies are growing, because they're offering what their customers see as great value. I think you offer great value. The boats I bought for my kids have stood up to almost 10 years of daily use. The kids never got tired of them. And almost every guest we've had who used our bathroom commented on the boats. They made people smile. I've lost track of how many of them I've given away, because I thought they were great value.

"So we can either retreat into a little hole, or we can go out and find more people who will have fun with these boats. I like the second option." Julie paused.

"Any other questions?" No one spoke.

"Great. My question for you is where should I stand so I'll get a good view of a lot of what goes on?"

There was some discussion, and eventually they agreed that the best option was to stand between the chop saw and the CNC machine. You could see most of the shop from there, but it wasn't where the forklift ran, so it was safe.

"Just remember your hearing protection and safety glasses," I reminded her.

Julie moved into position and just stood there until the break – 90 minutes. I didn't see her make a note the whole time, or use her phone. At the break she wandered over to my desk.

"What did you see?" I asked. "Bet you want to make a lot of changes!"

"Not right now. I don't understand enough. I don't even know what you think the problems in this area are, so that might be a good place to start. Do you want to take a short walk with me, and then you can take your break when the others get back? Would that be OK?"

A walk? In the middle of the work day? I didn't get it. I guess she saw my hesitation.

"It's OK," she said. "I often go for a walk when I want to mull things over or get some clarity. I also find it helps me communicate more easily with whoever I'm speaking. After all, we're going in the same direction when we're walking, and that's a good start." She smiled. I realized Julie smiled a lot. I'd have to watch that and see if it lasted. So I nodded. "Left, or right?" she asked as we reached the sidewalk.

"Just railway tracks and a shunt-yard to the left. It's often pretty noisy. But if we go right, there is a park about two blocks along. It backs onto a creek and there's a little footpath that's wide enough for two. It runs along the creek for a kilometre or so."

"Perfect."

And so we started out on the first of what would be many walks. Sometimes we got just as far as the park before we turned around. Sometimes, when the subject was tougher, we'd go the whole way to the end of the pathway. The weather never seemed to slow Julie down. But then I remembered, she'd grown up here; she knew that in this city you do what you want, and dress for the weather.

We walked in silence for a minute or so. I was going to let her take the lead.

"I saw a lot of walking," she started. "Back and forth. I'm not sure what it was for. Sometimes it looked like people needed a tool they didn't have. Sometimes they were off to ask a question. Some I have no idea why they were walking. It's not good or bad. It was just a lot of walking. If I was going to guess, I'd say a third of everyone's time was spent walking." She paused. We continued walking. Thirty seconds later, she asked, "Does that estimate fit for you?"

I'd never thought of it before. But when I let the images of the day play through my mind, I could see what she was getting at. "Yeah. That's not far off as a guess."

"So what is it about how we've set up their work that makes all that walking necessary?" The question dropped like a pebble into a pond, with ripples spreading out everywhere. I thought of all the people that come to me with questions. All the time people spent looking for tools and work orders or even for product. All the time the orders aren't clear. And the times that someone just forgot and left their water bottle behind and went back to pick it up. Yeah, there was a lot of walking.

I relayed this to Julie. "Keep that in mind," she advised. Our feet moved onto the crushed gravel of the pathway.

"What's the biggest problem in your area," she started again.

"Shouldn't we get back to the plant now?" I asked. "Break will be over in a couple of minutes and with us both away there won't be any supervisor."

"OK," she allowed, "I'll give you this today because it's my first day. In three months, I want you to trust the people on your team enough, and to have done your work well enough that they know what to do for the next several hours. You should be able to step away from your area for half a day anytime and have it function just fine without you. Don't worry about what you'll be doing... you'll be busy enough. But, to do that you need to trust your people, and have systems in place so they know what's next.

"What do you think is the role of the supervisor?"

I thought for a moment. "I guess it's to tell people what to do and solve any problems that come up so production goes out on time."

"That's a part of it," Julie countered. "To my mind, you have two things you have to do. Achieve the mission of the company, and look after your people. That's it. Everything else is what the religious writers call 'commentary'!" She laughed. "And there is a lot of commentary. But, if you keep those two things in mind, you'll always do well."

"Tell it back to me. What is the role of a supervisor."

"Something about the mission, and something about the people... um... oh, yeah, look after your people. But if I'm nice how do I get stuff done?"

"Who said anything about being nice?"

"You did," I retorted. "Look after your people."

"Looking after people and being nice are not the same thing," Julie commented. "Think about your family – who was your primary parent?"

"My mum, for sure. My dad died when I was 14."

"Sorry to hear that. Must have been a hard couple of years after that for you."

"Yup." I didn't want to go into it.

"So..." She paused. "Did your mum always let you do everything you wanted?"

"You kidding? She was pretty harsh sometimes."

"And did she have rules that bugged you?"

"M-hmm," I nodded my head as we walked.

"So your mum wasn't always 'nice,' but she looked after you... she looked out for you. That's what the rules were for. For us as supervisors it's just the same. We have to look after our people. And that means we often make decisions our people either don't understand or don't like. That's not a pass to be mean or arbitrary, but it sure doesn't mean that we'll always be nice or make decisions our people like.

"Like you and me. You won't like some of my decisions or some of the things I say to you. But I hope you will feel that I have your back, that I'm fair, and that I'm genuinely interested in helping you take your career wherever it is you want it to go. Of course, you won't be able to asses that until you've seen me function for a while.

"Now back to my question. What's the biggest problem you're facing right now in your area?"

I thought about it. I tend to think things through by talking, so I told Julie about Sylvie who has an attendance issue, and Marcus whose work is really inconsistent, and Zhou who has trouble producing quality work. But then it dawned on me that the real problem in my area was that our department wasn't able to consistently hit the timelines that Peter needed for delivery of the raw parts. And because of that, we were causing late shipments.

"Oh," I went on. "I'm just realizing that in terms of meeting our mission, when my department misses a delivery time, I've messed up."

"Yes. Exactly," Julie replied.

"So that's probably my biggest problem right now."

"Maybe, but maybe that's just your biggest symptom. Do you know why you're often late?"

"Not really," I said.

"Then that's what you need to work on."

We were almost back at the plant. The conversation moved on to weekend plans and other little stuff. Back at the plant we parted ways. I was surprised to see her walk right back to the same spot and begin watching again.

An hour and a half later I was working with Zhou trying to determine why some parts had been cut undersized. Julie came by and asked to speak to me. "When you're finished," she said. "You OK if I listen in while I wait?" She said it to Zhou as much as to me.

What was I going to say? She was my boss, so she could do what she liked. Still, this was different. Rocky never cared what you were doing when he had something to say. He came first. I don't know how many times I'd had to leave one of my team wondering what to do because Rocky came and interrupted.

Two minutes later, I'd finished with Zhou.

"How did that go?" she asked.

"OK, I guess. Zhou still has a hard time communicating in English, so I'm never sure if she actually got what I told her. You must have run into that before."

"Sure have," she replied. "It's a real problem, and I bet it's bigger here in the city. We didn't have so many people immigrate directly to the little town where I used to work, so most people could understand English fine. Reading and writing was another matter, but at least we didn't have speaking and listening issues."

"What was your objective in that exchange?" she went on.

"I just wanted Zhou to pay more attention to the fine adjustment of the stop. I know that if you measure it the wrong way it can make enough difference that the parts will come out wrong. Since we'll usually run a couple of hundred parts, it can lead to a lot of waste. Zhou makes that mistake a lot... we probably lose a couple of hundred parts every week."

"So what will Zhou do differently next time?"

"I want her to be more careful."

"OK. Are you interested in what I observed?"

"Sure."

"My bet is that Zhou won't do anything different next time. I'm guessing you don't have kids, but you mentioned you'd been a camp counsellor?"

"Yeah. One summer."

"Think back to that experience. I bet that those kids found a lot of ways to mess up your instructions, right?"

I nodded.

"So, if you tell a kid to 'be careful', do they have any idea what you mean?"

I paused. I thought I could see where this was going, and I was starting to feel uncomfortable.

"No," I started hesitantly, "They don't know what to look for."

"Exactly. So at camp I bet you got good at telling them what specific steps you wanted them to take. And probably got good pretty quickly or you wouldn't have survived. What behaviour you want, not what attitude. Is this making sense?"

I stood, listening.

"Your staff is just the same. No, they're not kids. But if they're not doing something you want, then my first bet is they either don't know what you want, or they don't know how. Either way, they don't know what to look for. So you have to be specific."

"But that will take more time, won't it?" I replied.

"Will it?" she asked.

"Of course it will," I said irritated. "Just makes sense. If I have to explain in gory detail it's going to take way longer."

"Will it really?" she repeated.

I looked at her. I was thinking this could get annoying. If she didn't like what I was doing, she should just say so and tell me what to do.

"You seem to want a different answer, so tell me what you want me to say."

Julie took a breath. "We'll leave it for now. But over the rest of today I want you to consider the impact of being quick in your instructions, compared to being detailed. You might even try some experiments. You could give one person some instructions in detail and see what results you get, and then give instructions quickly to someone else and see what happens."

"Come and find me at the end of the day and tell me what you found."

***

By the end of the day I was exhausted. Julie had got me thinking. I was feeling like I was a complete beginner again. How was it that I hadn't seen the walking? How was it that I wasn't crystal clear about the biggest problem in my area?

She was expecting so much from me – and the others, too, I guessed. How could I ever just walk away from my area for half a day. I couldn't imagine it. And how could I take so much time that my instructions were crystal clear? I didn't have that much time.

But I did try what she asked, and gave some detailed instructions to Sylvie, and then I gave some really quick directions to Jas. I realized looking back that Jas had come back to me with a question about her work within 5 minutes, and then again half an hour later. But I hadn't seen Sylvie move from her machine. I headed over to where she was working.

"How's it going?" I asked easily.

"Just fine," she responded. "I think I should get these parts done before the end of the shift," she went on. I was surprised but didn't say anything. I wasn't expecting the parts until mid-morning the next day, early morning if I was lucky.

"That's great. What happened to make it go so easily?" I asked.

"Dunno," she started. "It just seemed like I had answers to my questions. I noticed you took way longer to tell me what to do, and I kind of wondered why. But I like the way it came out. I could just focus on my work."

"Great. Thanks for the feedback. Got anything fun planned for tonight?"

"Yeah." Her eyes lit up. "Me and my boyfriend – we're going to ballroom dance class tonight. I told him that I wanna be able to dance at my wedding. He surprised me and bought us lessons. It was so sweet." I smiled at her. "No, no. It's not like that. We're not gett'n married or anything. He's just my boyfriend."

I smiled again. "Have fun anyway." I headed off to the offices to find Julie.

***

Julie looked up and smiled as I entered her office. "Well, what did you find?"

I told Julie about the two experiences with Jas and Sylvie.

"Well, given that experience, do you still think it takes longer to give instructions in detail?"

I had to admit that it was probably a lot closer to even than I'd thought. And, I noticed, Sylvie was way more productive in the last hour of the day than Jas, and they're pretty much the same as far as being good workers.

Maybe there was something to what Julie was pushing for.

Reflecting on the Chapter

For Supervisors

- What are the challenges in your area?
- If you were to walk through your area for the first time, what do you think you would notice?
- How are you giving your instructions to your team members? Are you rushing, or taking time?
- Which one of the current challenges in your area is having the biggest impact on performance?

Actions to Take

- Stand in one place in your area and watch. The first time you do it, take one hour. Make a point of observing for the full hour before you move. Don't make any notes while you're watching. Make sure you tell your team in advance what you're doing and why. Make any notes you want after the hour.
- After you have observed, ask your team members about your observations. Use curiosity, rather than accusation. They're probably doing the best they know. Ask, "I noticed <state observation>. How does doing it that way help you get your job done?"
- Review the Assigning Work instruction and try it out.

For Managers (you have supervisors reporting to you)

Consider all the questions for supervisors for yourself. Then consider the following.

- What are the challenges that each of your supervisors face in their area?
- What are the challenges you face for your area of responsibility?

Actions to Take

- Which one of the current challenges in your area is having the biggest impact on performance?
- Stand in one place in each of the areas you are responsible for and watch. The first time you do it, take one hour. Make a point of observing for the full hour before you move. Make notes only at the end of the hour.

■ After you have observed, speak to the supervisor of the area about your observations. Use curiosity, rather than accusation. The crew members are probably doing the best they know. Ask, "I noticed <state observation>. How does doing it that way help your crew get their job done?" Then go with them to the individual crew members.

■ Review the Assigning Work instruction and try it out.

Techniques for Better Performance

Assigning Work

This six-step system will increase the effectiveness of your work assignments. One supervisor started using this and within a week he had eliminated five hours of overtime a week because his crew did not have to spend time looking for him. Another started using it and found the error rate of his crew went down by 50% because they were not guessing about the information they didn't have.

Important Step	Key Point	Reason
1. Tell them early	• Before they finish previous task • End of previous shift is ideal	They can keep going People aren't waiting for assignments at start of shift
2. Assign enough tasks	• Enough to keep them busy until you return plus ½ hour, or • Enough to keep the constraint operation busy plus ½ hour, whichever is greater • Include a small task	So they don't spend time looking for you So the constraint operation doesn't run out of work For end of the shift

3. Communicate **WHAT** and **HOW**	• What – be specific
	• How
	  – Safety specific to job
	  – Special instructions
	  – Non-normal tolerances
	  – Tooling and material to use
	  – Who can help them
		Prevents confusion
		Makes them aware of what is out of the ordinary

4. Ask how long they think it will take, uninterrupted	• Negotiate if their estimate is unreasonable – either way • Don't let them underestimate or rush	Their input is a commitment Rushing creates mistakes and increases safety risk
5. Tell them **WHEN** it is due	• Get them help or reassign work to meet deadline if needed	Meeting deadline is supervisor's responsibility
6. Ask them to summarize	• Listen for specifics of what, how and when	Guarantees they know what you need done

You can get your own copy of this at www.becomingthesupervisor.com/downloads.

Chapter 6

The Morning Meeting

Two weeks later, Peter came to me late in the morning.

"Look, Trevor, you've got to do something with Sunil. If I don't get some of the tug parts into the hands of my crew we're going to miss the deadline for the Seabrook order. It's a big deal for the company. No way I can do the assembly if I don't have the parts. I've talked to Sunil but he's adamant that he has to get the bulk carrier parts done first. I don't know why. Those orders are due way later, and I think he's just avoiding the tug parts because they're smaller and fussier to work on. Tell him to get to work on the tug."

I told him I'd look into it. When I talked to Sunil, he told me that he knew about the tug parts, but he was in the middle of a big run of the bulk carrier parts. They had a really tricky set-up, he explained, and if he broke the set-up to deal with Peter's request, he figured the per-piece cost of those parts was going to go through the roof. "You don't want things to cost more, do you?" he asked.

I admitted that, no, I didn't want costs to go up. I'd seen last month's numbers, and between some rework and some shipping errors, we'd made money, but barely. Tight enough that two or three double set-ups would have erased any profit. "Leave it with me," I put him off. "I'll get back to you late today or first thing tomorrow."

I found Julie just after lunch. "I really need ten minutes of your time for some advice, Julie. And I need it before the end of the day or I'm going to have a war in my department."

"See you at 2:15," she answered. "I will have just ten minutes. I'm taking my mum to a late appointment and I need to be driving by 2:30."

I was at her office at 2:10. Three minutes later she walked in. I'm still not sure how she does that. All the things she has going on, and she's still always a few minutes ahead of schedule.

I described my problem. "So you see," I wrapped up, "it's like they're not on the same team. They have no idea what the priorities are for anyone else, or for the company."

"And whose problem is that?" she asked. A bald, uncomfortable question because there was only one answer, which I didn't like.

"Mine, I guess."

"Yup," she said. "So when do you talk through your priorities with your team?"

"What do you mean?" I asked.

"Hmm…" She lingered over her thoughts. "Before I say anything, let me ask some questions. Do you hold a daily huddle? Maybe you call it a stand-up meeting, or a morning meeting."

"No. What's that?"

"That's the answer I thought I'd get," Julie responded slowly. "Did Rocky ever meet with the team to talk about what was coming up next?"

"I think there might have been one or two meetings like that. There was one time when a big order was coming in and he wanted everyone to give it priority over everything. And a couple of times Mrs. K called all the staff together for some announcement or other. But daily? No way."

"Trevor," she went on, "when you were doing production, how did you know what your priorities were?"

I thought for a minute. "Umm. Most of the time I guessed. Usually I took whatever had been sitting in the queue for my station the longest. Unless Rocky came over and told me to do something different. Sometimes, if I was unsure, I'd walk around to find him and ask him what next. He seemed to like it when I did that. Some days I'd lose half an hour just walking around trying to find him if I had to do it three or four times."

"I bet it slowed you down a bit," she commented.

"You bet. Like I said, sometimes I lost half an hour in a day."

"And how do your team members know what to do next, and what their priorities should be?"

"I tell them," I answered. "They're pretty good about finding me and asking what next."

"How much time do they spend doing that?"

I thought for a minute. "I guess most of them come to talk to me at least a couple of times a day. So that might take 2 to 3 minutes if I'm there in the department, but if I'm somewhere else in the plant it could be 10 minutes, easily. So…"

"We're talking at least 5 to 7 minutes each time, aren't we?" she interjected.

"Easily," I answered. "I guess that would add up to 15 minutes a day per person – maybe 20, and I have seven people on my team, so maybe two hours in total."

"And a lot of that is waste as they look for you, isn't it?" she went on.

"Oh yeah," I agreed.

"Here's what I'd like to explore with you," she said. "What would happen if you took all that time that you're using anyway, and brought everyone together once a day to go over the priorities for the day? Rather than fritter the time away a bit at a time, if you bring everyone together, everyone gets the same story and the benefit is you only have to say it once!"

"I guess it might help…" I started. "But every time I've seen a crew get together it just winds up being a bitching session, and there's no value. At least that's all I've ever seen." By this time I'd seen Julie operating long enough to know that she rarely floated an idea that she had any questions about. Either she'd seen it working somewhere, or she's used it herself, or she knew someone who had.

"You're right," she replied. "So you will need a pretty solid and tight agenda, and it will take some practice. You'll be interested that Gil in shipping was talking to me about the same problem just two weeks ago. So it's time."

"For what?" I asked.

"For me to start my morning meetings," she replied, with such an ordinary tone that it caught me off guard. I figured it would be something that I'd need to do, not something from her. "Starting on Monday, you and the other department leads will meet with me every morning for 14 minutes at 9:05. Plan around it. This isn't optional. I'll be sending out calendar invitations tomorrow after I've spoken with everyone. The invitation will have the agenda.

"As for your team, you'll see how this helps address your problem within a week. But that doesn't help with today's problem. How often do you make those bulk carrier parts with the tricky set-up?"

"Probably once a month. And because they're so tricky, once they get it set up, we run about a month's supply. We have a bit of flex because we plan to run them with still about two week's inventory on hand."

"How long do the set-ups take?" Julie asked.

"I haven't timed it," I answered. I was learning that Julie always wanted measured data. "When I last did the job it took me over two hours."

"OK." Julie seemed to be clear in her mind. "What would *you* do right now regarding those bulk carrier parts and the tug parts?"

I waffled. "Well, we need the parts for both," I said, "and we really don't want the extra costs for the set-ups, so I think I'd let Sunil finish the bulk carrier parts, and then do the tug parts."

Julie looked at me carefully. "I'm going to make a decision that I'm not excited about, but it needs to be made, especially given the hours we're talking about. It's a general principal about priorities. If you have to choose between making a shipment on time, and doing other stuff, make the shipment on time unless there is a cost impact of more than $300. I want to hear about it each time you make one of those decisions – either way. Not because I'll second guess you, but because I need to know where you're facing challenges.

"In this case, the cost impact is about 3 hours of work – an extra tear-down and set-up. The cost impact is under the $300 threshold, so shipment on time wins. So get Sunil to make the change and get those tug parts done. If you bring the team together for a short meeting at ..." She paused to look at her calendar. "let's say 8:15 tomorrow morning – I'll explain to them why we made that decision. Do you get why we made that decision?"

"Yeah."

"OK. I have to go now. Get Sunil to make the change and tell him we're going to explain the decision to everyone tomorrow. At eight I want to meet with you and have you explain to me why we made that decision. Then we'll meet with your team at 8:15. Good?"

I nodded and she dashed out to her car.

Sunil grumbled a bit, but by the end of the shift the first tug parts were coming out.

The next morning at 8 Julie asked me to explain the decision.

"Well," I started, "The issue is that we don't want to be late for our customers, so we'll do whatever it takes to get them their products."

"Good try," she responded. "Not the whole story, but a good start. We need to make three points:

1. We are in business to serve our customers, so our test is always, 'Can we meet our customers' requirements while making some profit?' We don't serve our customers if we go out of business. But we won't have them back if we're late.
2. $300 represents the average margin we make on our orders so even if meeting the order costs us $300, we don't lose money. It's not perfect, but it will be close enough often enough that it's useful. Other plants will use a different number, but for us, this will work.
3. I want to hear about it because if a problem comes up regularly, then we need to fix it. In this case, it sounds like the set-up time is an issue, but we won't fix that in a day, so we just have to eat the cost of the extra set-up – at least this time.

So, let's hear you try to explain it again."

I did much better the second time around. Apparently she thought so too, because she let me explain it to the team at 8:15. I saw several heads nod, and Sunil told me that now he got why we made the decision.

Later in the morning Julie's invitation arrived in my in-box. There was the agenda (Table 6.1).

Table 6.1　The Agenda for the Morning Meetings

Start time 9:05
Latest finish time 9:19
Agenda
1. Five wins
2. Yesterday's results
3. Today's priorities
4. Obstacles to meet today's priorities
5. Today's experiments/improvement work
6. Safety
7. Company stuff – if any

I was intrigued. It didn't seem that difficult. I figured the biggest challenge was going to be keeping it to 14 minutes.

I thought about it and decided to try something.

Right after lunch, I called the team together.

"I want to take 10 minutes to make sure we're on the same page," I started. "The last couple of days have been a bit of a scramble."

"No kidding," Sunil smirked.

"Yeah," I went on, "which is why I'm trying this. Here's what we need to deliver today and tomorrow." I ran through a list of a dozen parts that would be needed in assembly by the end of the next day. "Does anyone see any obstacles to achieving this?"

"Yeah," Marcus piped up. He was usually really quiet. "I don't have the raw material I need for two of those parts. We were supposed to have the scrap sized and ready yesterday, but there's no sign of it being delivered yet, and we're just hoping that there aren't any surprises."

"OK," I said. "Thanks. I'll pursue that once we're finished. Anything else?"

"I'm not sure I can get all of the cabin parts for the freighters done by the end of tomorrow," Sylvie said in her usual quiet way.

"What's up?" I asked.

"Well the machine doesn't seem to be running smoothly, and I've noticed some of the parts aren't in tolerance. I haven't been able to figure out why."

"OK. I'll have our millwright come over and have a look at it with you. Is there another way to make the parts?" I knew there was. I'd done it. But Sylvie didn't know that.

"Yes. We can run them in two stages on the other two machines. There will be no problem with tolerances, but I'd need another person to help me run the drill press."

"OK. We'll sort out that schedule after the meeting. Sunil, please carry on with your current task, but when you finish that, see if you can help Sylvie. Anything else from anyone?"

There was silence. "Great. Thanks everyone. And let me know if you run into any other issues with those work orders."

Less than two minutes later everyone was on their way back to their workstations. I called Sally in purchasing and explained the situation. "Can you please find out what's up and when we will see that delivery, Sally? We need it here by 3 today to meet our deadlines. It was supposed to be here yesterday." She said she'd do what she could. "Thanks, Sally. You're a saviour."

Then I walked over to where I knew our millwright was working on a new guard. "How's it going, Jamie?" I started.

"Good," she replied. She didn't use a lot of words. Ever.

"What's your biggest obstacle, Jamie?" I asked.

"No place for a bolt here." She gestured.

Jamie was very resourceful. I knew she'd figure it out so I carried on.

"Any idea when you'll be at a point you can stop for a few minutes? Sylvie's having some difficulty with her machine and I'd like you to have a look at it. She said it wasn't staying in tolerance."

"Give me 20 minutes," Jamie said.

"Thanks so much. Let me know what you find."

"Sure."

And I was on my way. Later that day she reported that one of the adjustment screws was partially stripped, which was why the machine wouldn't hold its setting. She figured she could fix it in about 15 minutes, but she needed a part, and figured if she ordered it this afternoon, she'd have it all dealt with by the end of the next day. In the meantime, she'd put in a temporary fix. I thanked her and crossed that one off my list.

The next morning at 9:05 all the supervisors were standing around outside Julie's office. It occurred to me that three months ago there might have been one or two of us. Julie's attention to being punctual was clearly having an impact.

In the next 12 minutes we went through her whole agenda. I was clear about what orders had priority, and realized I would need to swap the sequence of two orders in my schedule. I'd be telling my team later in the morning.

At the end, Julie asked, "Well… was that useful?" Positive noises all around. "Good. We'll be doing this daily. I'm open to your suggestions to make this work better. And today I want you to notice how many times you rely on the information you learned at this meeting." We all headed off to our areas.

Later that morning, right after break, I pulled everyone together. I had Julie's agenda taped to my day book. It went OK. No one had any wins to offer. But once I'd set out the priorities for the day and asked if there were any questions, Marcus asked about a problem he had machining a part last time, and he had that part on his list for tomorrow. Jas offered a suggestion that had worked for her when she did that job; Marcus said he would try that. Then they were all away, clearly uncomfortable with the whole process.

However, I noticed that during the afternoon I had only one question about priorities. Normally I'd have had half a dozen. Maybe there was something to this.

The next day we repeated the process. Again, no one volunteered any wins.

"Come on everyone. Didn't anything go right yesterday? We're not asking for 'save the planet' wins – just something we got right."

"I saw Steve throw his earplugs in the garbage," Giles cracked. Sniggers all around.

"I think it's a win when people put stuff where it belongs. And if that's not what they normally do, even better." I knew Steve had a bit of reputation as a slob.

"Oh," came the reply. It was clear Giles was a bit disappointed that his jab at Steve hadn't got more of a rise.

As the days went on, the meetings got easier and easier. People knew what to expect. We heard about all sorts of little wins – a jig that was adjusted to fit better, a part that was adjusted in design just a millimetre but it let us use the raw material more efficiently, a part that ran correctly on the first piece, a shield that eliminated some waste on the floor, and so on.

Three weeks later there was a bit of a catastrophe. Well, that's too strong a word. But I was pretty annoyed. Wood had arrived, but it had far more flaws than usual. When the tools hit the wood, it would often splinter. It took two of the crew an extra three hours to get the production done and delivered. That stuff happens. But when I heard late in the day that three people in the team knew about the impending problem but didn't say anything, I was furious.

At the next day's meeting I asked if there were any quality issues with incoming material. I heard someone choke down a laugh. I lost it. "Really? People knew about it and didn't say anything? That's almost as bad as deliberately breaking stuff or passing bad work on to the next person. It's disrespectful to your co-workers and our owner." I was on a rant. And I didn't have a graceful way out. The crew seemed to slide back, avoiding my eyes, wanting my tirade to end. I didn't know how to stop without looking like a jerk. But of course, that's what I was at that moment.

Fortunately, I was pretty much through the morning meeting. I turned and walked away. The crew milled around for a few moments and then I guess they all went off to their workstations.

Later that morning, I got a message that Julie wanted to see me. Not a surprise. "What happened?" she asked. I was surprised because there was no anger in her voice.

I described the situation.

"Were you happy with the outcome?"

"Of course not," I said bitterly.

"So how else could you have made your point?"

I didn't know what to say.

"Look," Julie tried again, "You didn't like the result. Whatever you did wasn't working for you. But you had a real problem. So, what will you do differently next time? Because there will be a next time."

Again, I had no idea how to respond. She was silent waiting for me; it seemed to go on for ages. Clearly, I'd need to say something or the silence would just keep going.

"I really don't know how else to deal with it," I offered.

"Good," Julie said. "If you can admit it, that's a start. Do you want a suggestion?"

"Please," I answered.

"OK. In this situation, where you have heard that someone knew but you don't know who, it's appropriate to ask in the group context. I would start by saying what you know. You received a shipment that had a lot of flaws. It wasn't caught at the formal inspection and that's a different issue to deal with at another time. It took two people an extra three hours to process the wood, and added $0.50 to each part made from that wood.

"Then tell them that you overheard comments that indicated some folks not part of QA had noticed the problem but hadn't said anything. We could have avoided the problem, but we didn't, because no-one said anything.

"Those are the facts that we know. Then you have a couple of options. You could ask who knew, or you could say, 'I don't know who knew, but I need you all to be very clear about my expectation. If you notice something that could cost us a lot of time, what should you do?' Then, if someone gets the answer right, you can reinforce it. And if they don't get it quite right, you can correct them. If no-one gets it, you will have to tell them directly. Do you have a preference for one of the approaches?" She waited for my response.

I thought about it. "I think I like the first option better. I want to know who didn't say anything. Then I can deal with whoever it is."

"Hmmm…" Then Julie paused. I was learning that when she paused, it was often because she was thinking about how to correct where I was headed. On the other hand, it's way better than Rocky, who would say nothing or blow up, neither of which helped.

"I have two questions," she started. "First, how many people were there that didn't say anything. Second, what would you do to 'deal with' whoever it was?"

"Well," I started, "I heard there were two or three. And I guess I'd just like to look them in the eye and say, 'Really?'"

"What do you remember about our conversations about mistakes in the crew," Julie asked.

"Not sure what you mean?"

"If one or two people have messed up, do you talk to the whole crew, or the specific individuals?"

Then I got her point. Julie had consistently told us that she didn't want us talking to the group if there were just one or two offenders. She wanted us to do the hard work of confronting the individuals.

"I guess, really, I should go find out who it was and talk to the individuals."

"And what will your conversation be?"

"I guess I need to find out what they knew, and what they thought they were supposed to do."

"OK. Do that and you'll learn some of the details. Then what?"

"Well, I suppose if no one knew that they should say something, then I can talk to the whole group, and if they do know but didn't do anything, then I can address that."

"Sounds like a plan to me," Julie said. "A much better plan than you started with. Get on with it." She paused. "One other thing. I think you owe your crew an apology. Even if you are right, they need more respect than you showed. Let me know how it goes."

So I did. It didn't take long to find out who knew. I had my suspicions just because of where it was in the production process. When I talked with the two individuals, I learned that with Rocky, anyone who said anything about a problem was treated as someone whining about their work, rather than someone being helpful.

The next day, at the morning meeting I apologized. I told them what I'd learned. I explained that I want them to say something when they see a situation that will cost us money. It was hard facing the crew and apologizing. But I must have done OK, because later in the day, Marcus came looking for me.

"Never seen that before… a boss apologizing," he said. "Maybe you won't be such a bad boss after all."

After that, I felt like I was floating.

Over time the morning meetings got smoother and smoother. The crew knew what to expect and they were prepared. I started keeping a list of the wins each day, and it got to be pretty impressive as the weeks went by. I found that I had fewer and fewer interruptions to my day, and fewer and fewer situations that "emerged" from the floor because the crew were identifying them in advance.

Reflecting on the Chapter

For Supervisors

■ How do your crew members know what their priorities are?
■ How much of the confusion and conflict in your area happens because priorities are not clear?
■ Are your decision guidelines clear when priorities conflict?
■ Have you had the experience of members of your crew not speaking up? Have you wondered why they might be hesitant to say something?

Actions to Take

■ Compare the agenda of your daily meeting with Julie's. Is there something you could add to yours? Is there something you could remove?
■ Try out daily meetings for two weeks. Tell your team it is an experiment. If daily meetings aren't normal in your workplace, start small, with one win from the day before, and the priorities for today's and tomorrow's production. Ask them at the end of each week what they think. Notice any changes to your interruptions.

For Managers (you have supervisors reporting to you)

Consider all the questions for supervisors for yourself. Then consider the following.

■ How do your supervisors know what the company's priorities are?
■ Do any of your supervisors have difficulties with priorities? Do they need some assistance or help to learn how to communicate priorities?

Actions to Take

■ Attend the daily meetings of each of your supervisors on a regular basis. Simply observe. Then afterwards, review any observations with them. Focus only on the key points (see table next page) to start. Then, over time, as they get better, offer feedback on refining details.

Techniques for Better Performance

Daily Meetings

This daily meeting agenda should take 12–15 minutes, no more.

Use this agenda and these guidelines to keep it crisp.

Allow clarifying questions, but don't use this time for long explanations. If someone wants detailed information, schedule a time to respond. Check how many others are interested, and if needed, schedule a short meeting for the one topic.

Agenda Item	Key Points	Reasons
1. Five wins	■ Just the results, not how ■ Any small gain	Keep it short Reinforces that small wins are OK
2. Yesterday's results	■ Graph it before the meeting ■ 3–4 key metrics that you are following for the group	Visual is memorable, and faster Keeps the team focused
3. Today's priorities	■ Specific orders that need to move to next department by end of day ■ Key orders for tomorrow	Everyone has the same story Lets people anticipate needs
4. Ask for obstacles for today's priorities	■ List them only ■ Solve them after the meeting	Keeps the meeting moving and you can set better priorities Doesn't use up the time of people who aren't involved
5. Today's experiments or improvement work	■ State the specific activity for the day	Lets people anticipate the impact on production, and what they need to work around
6. Safety	■ Review any incidents from last day ■ Highlight any new concerns	Lets everyone understand countermeasures Keeps everyone aware
7. Company announcements	■ As you are informed by your boss ■ No speculation	Keeps your team in the loop Prevents rumours

You can download a copy of this form at www.becomingthesupervisor.com/downloads.

Chapter 7

He Quit – Learning to Instruct

A few weeks later on Thursday, I was just getting ready to leave when Steve stuck his head in the door. That was a surprise. Steve never stuck around. At the end of his shift he was gone within minutes. He didn't speed away or squeal his tires, but he didn't linger. So, if he was poking his head in my door 5 minutes after quitting time, something was up.

He was clearly feeling a bit uncomfortable as he told me that he'd found a better job and wanted to give his notice. He knew that two weeks' notice was usual, but was hoping I'd be OK if he left at the end of the next week – six days' notice.

What was I going to say? If I made him stay the full two weeks he'd be frustrated and his mind wouldn't be on his work. And he was going, one way or the other, so I was going to have to deal with him not being around eventually. An extra four days wasn't going to significantly change my situation. So I agreed he could go at the end of the next week.

So that was that. I thought I should probably get someone in, but I knew we didn't have a lot of orders waiting. I figured I'd have time to find someone and get the person up to speed. Since I'd never had to hire anyone before, I wasn't sure what to do, but I had a few days to come up with a plan.

Things didn't work out so well.

The next week, Steve's last, we got two big orders – one from a new customer and one from one of our "A" customers. Mrs. Kumar had made it very clear that there were two sorts of orders that she always wanted to be out on time: orders for "A" customers and first time orders. Our "A" customers each represented more than 4% of our sales; between them, they represented over 60% of our total. Both orders also came with very short timelines – doable, but short.

When the orders came in, I did my usual check to make sure that we had sufficient material on hand (we did), and looked at the loading on our two critical machines. We should have been fine. Except that the next day, two things happened. First, Zhou cut 300 pieces too small. And second, our drill press broke. A bearing on the spindle failed, so the drill tip was wandering around like a drunk leaving a tavern. It was going to take two days to get a replacement.

Normally, neither of these issues would have been a problem: we'd have used the older, more manual tools, and I'd have got people to do a bit of overtime. But with Steve gone, these measures weren't going to be enough. We would be late on at least one of the orders, and maybe both.

I went in to see Julie to ask her about the situation.

"It does sound like you have a problem," she commented after I told her the situation. Then she was quiet. I was puzzled. There was no explosion. No raised voice. Nothing that I'd learned to expect from Rocky. Just an observation that *I* had a problem. Not what I thought! I thought *she* had a problem. Maybe she did, but she sure wasn't letting it show.

"So what are *you* going to do," she asked, "and do you have any obstacles to getting it done?"

"I don't know – on either count."

Julie leaned toward me. "I'm very disappointed, Trevor." Her voice was very quiet. I shrank in my seat. She went on. "I don't mind that you run into stuff you don't know how to handle. That happens all the time. Happens to me, too. But I'm not happy that you knew for four days that Steve was leaving, that it was going to create a problem, and that you didn't ask for help. You're in your position to solve problems, not ignore them. I don't expect you to have all the answers. None of us has all the answers. But I do expect you not to ignore stuff you don't know how to handle. I expect better from you. And I know you can do it." She stopped.

I'd seen her do this before. She'd tell me what she expected, made it clear how my actions (or in this case inaction) had been inadequate, and then she'd wait for me to say something. It felt really uncomfortable, but I was starting to see that every time she did that, I'd answer her, and learn something.

"I'm sorry," I started, and paused.

"So am I," she said flatly. Ouch.

"I just had so much going on that needed attention right away, and I thought I could think about it for a few days. I didn't expect to have to deal with a mistake and a failed piece of equipment."

Julie waited. Said nothing. I couldn't believe how terrible I felt when she did that. It was way worse than Rocky blowing up. As I look back on it, I can see that she was leaving me with the consequences of my action. The thing about Rocky was, you knew that he'd blow up, but then he'd take over, do what needed doing, and you could go back to life as normal. But when Julie was quiet like that, I wound up thinking about all the ways I'd messed up, and things I could have done differently. It made me consider alternatives. But in the moment, I felt like I was frozen. Then, I realized Julie was still waiting.

"Sorry, Julie. I clearly messed up. And I don't have a way to fix it – at least not that I can see. I can get some overtime from the crew, and if it was just the mistake, or just the machine, we could probably have skated through, but with both – I just don't see how we can do it..." I trailed off.

"I see." Julie started. "Let me start by saying thank you for acknowledging that you messed up. You did. And I'm glad you see it. We can work from that. So let's work together to see if we can solve the immediate problem, and then we can come back to the bigger issue – bigger for us long term, but not bigger for our customers. For them, their orders ARE the big issue."

Over the next 15 minutes, Julie pushed and prodded, looking for options and alternatives for every part of the operation. At the end we had a plan. I knew of a small wood shop in the next complex and they had the capability to redo the pieces Zhou had messed up. I'd make a call to see if they could fit our work into their day. It would cost more than us doing it ourselves, but not much more than us doing it on overtime. If they could get it done in 24 hours, then the rest of the plant could be lined up to get that order handled right away. For the broken drill press, I knew that there was an exact duplicate of our machine across town. They could use our tooling and jigs to make the parts correctly. Again, it would be more expensive than us doing the work, but still worth it to hit our deadline and avoid expedited freight. My second call would be to see if they could free up 4 hours of machine time for us. If so, then we could take part of that order to them, while we worked on the rest of it here. That would keep our team productive, and still let us meet our deadlines without unduly stressing the rest of the plant. Ten minutes later, I was two for two – it was going to work. I got our team onto the task of loading parts and material and tooling. While they did that, I lined up the deliveries.

I reported back to Julie, and she seemed happy enough. "Please come and see me at 3."

"OK," I replied, not entirely sure what would happen.

"See you then." Her head went down and she was back at whatever she was doing. Her ability to switch tasks and still be personable when she was talking to me was uncanny.

I was at her office just before 3.

The conversation started with identifying the big issue – I had a hole in my staff, but I didn't have a clear idea of the skills my staff already had, or what I needed. I also didn't know anything about how to train them. Then Julie got me to back up one more step. "Ok. You've identified two things you need to deal with. But what is your target? What state are you trying to achieve?"

I was puzzled. I needed to know what training my staff required, and I needed to know how to train. What more was there?

But with a few questions, Julie helped me see that these were solutions, ways to solve a problem. I wasn't really after the training – I wanted enough people to have enough skills that we'd always be able to produce, even if one or two of my team were suddenly unavailable. I had to have enough resilience in my staff that it didn't matter to the company if someone didn't show up, or a machine broke down. Training was just a way to get there.

That made sense. Training was a way to solve my problem. I still needed to know what training my team needed, and I still needed to know how. That hadn't changed. But now I had a clearer idea of why I was doing it.

Julie pushed me to come up with more obstacles to my target. At the end, my list looked like this.

TARGET – Always able to produce, regardless of staff absences

- Not enough people knew the drill press or the CNC
- Short one person with Steve leaving
- No inventory of what people know
- No training program
- Don't know what is essential to know at each operation
- Little documentation about how to do different operations
- Finicky machines that need a "special touch" makes them hard to learn

It was clear to me that I had to hire a replacement for Steve. In Julie's terms, I had two big obstacles. One was that I didn't have enough people for the work we had. The second was that I didn't have my people well enough trained.

But which one first?

"Do you really have the option of choosing?" Julie asked. "I agree that you can't do two things at the exact same moment. But if you got everyone trained up the way you want, would you have achieved your target?"

"No," I responded, "because I still wouldn't have enough people." Suddenly I could see where she was going with this. "And," I continued, "if I hired some-one to replace Steve, but didn't do the training I'd still have my basic problem."

"Exactly."

I decided that if I got the hiring process started, I could turn to the train-ing problem while I waited for people to start responding to my recruiting efforts.

Julie agreed. She inquired whether I'd ever hired before. I hadn't. She offered to handle the hiring for me. Her concern was that both needed doing, and that if I needed to learn both, she thought I should learn the training stuff first. She thought it was a more fundamental skill for anyone in a supervisory role; we'd focus on that.

Julie got me started working out a plan. We created a table with my team members along one side, and all the tasks that had to be done across the other (Figure 7.1).

We started filling it in.

"Look," Julie explained, "lots of people have lots of different ways to fill these training plans in. There isn't a right and a wrong way. Like some people call it a training matrix. I don't care what you call it. It's a tool to help you solve a problem. But I'll tell you how I did it, and why. I think it works. I'd like you to do it that way until you've used it for two months. Don't change anything. But talk to me after you've used it for two months. I'm sure you'll have some ideas for how it can be even more useful for you. I think it is important to do things in a way you know works and get that nailed before you start experimenting. Otherwise you don't really have a point of comparison. Can you go along with that?"

What could I say? It seemed pretty reasonable. I thought about when I was a kid learning soccer. Our coach had insisted when we started that we always pass the ball three times before anyone in the team shot at the net. By the middle of the season we had got so good at passing that we didn't have to run nearly as much as the other team; we would pass instead.

Training Matrix for Sussex Creek Boatworks																			DATE	YYYY/MM/DD	TOTAL CAPABILITY
Task																					
Procedure or work instruction reference - if none indicate		None	None	None	None	None	None	None	None	None	None	None	None	None	None	None	None	None			
Name	Job Description and reference																				Now
	Raw Stock																				0
	Raw Stock																				0
	Raw Stock																				0
	Raw Stock																				0
	Raw Stock																				0
	Raw Stock																				0
	Raw Stock																				0
	Raw Stock																				0
																					0
Currently Capable (Levels 3 & 4)		0	0	0	0	0	0	0	0	0	0	0	0	0	0	0	0	0			
Key		● = Level 4 (can instruct) ◕ = Level 3 (on own) ◑ = Level 2 (with supervision) ◔ = Level 1 (in training) ○ = Level 0 (needs to be trained)																				
Shading Indicates urgent need to ensure company capability																					

Figure 7.1   Julie's template for a training matrix.

So when the opportunity to run happened we were fresher. And we'd got so much better at putting the ball where we wanted, that we found that our shots on goal were more accurate, too. It was a good season. My mind drifted to the fun we had.

"Trevor?" Julie asked. "You still here?"

I started, and brought myself back to the moment. "Yeah. Sure. I can do that."

So she explained how she used circles filled in at different levels.

■ No circle – Doesn't need the training
■ Empty circle – Needs the skill, but training not completed
■ Quarter filled – Trained, but not ready to do it without close oversight
■ Half filled – Can do task on own, but needs supervision for complex jobs
■ Three-quarter filled – Can do task reliably on own for all jobs
■ Completely filled – Able to teach the task

She explained that using the circles with the quarters filled in as people gained skills provided an immediate visual indication of where the gaps are, and which ones need attention. She also noted that in her experience, when the table was posted people seemed more eager to learn more skills. They begin to see that if they know more, they'll be more valuable to the company.

She challenged me to complete the table over the next two days.

When I met her again, I had a revised table (Figure 7.2). She seemed pleased.

"Did you have any trouble completing the table?" she asked. It had been pretty straight-forward. But I did have one issue.

I explained my difficulty. "So you see, I have two big gaps, and both of them could hurt us. One of them already has. So I'm not sure which to pick. The drill press is important and both Jas and Sylvie can run it and do it well, and I know Zhou has been learning some of the simpler tasks but she's not ready to set it up on her own. Marcus can run it, but the quality is pretty shaky. Then there is the CNC. Really, it is only Sunil that can run it. Teyjas has tried, but can't be relied on for everything. He doesn't understand a lot of the complexities."

"Sounds like you have a fairly good handle on the situation. What is your target?"

Training Matrix for Sussex Creek Boatworks DATE YYYY/MM/DD

Task		Forklift	Receive Offcuts	Receive Goods	Planer	Planer - Change Blade	Jointer	Jointer - Change Blade	Chop Saw	Chop Saw - Change B	CNC Milling Machine Operate	CNC Milling Machine Set up	Pallet Jack	Band Saw	Finger Jointer	Drill Press	React Work Order		TOTAL CAPABILITY
Procedure or work instruction reference - if none indicate		None	None	None	None	None	None	None	None	None	None		None	None	None	None	None	None	
Name	**Job Description and reference**																		**Now**
Marcus	Raw Stock	◕	◕	◕	◕	◑	◕	◑	◕	◕			◕			◑	◑		8
Jas	Raw Stock	◑	◕	◕									◕	◕	◕	◕	●		7
Giles	Raw Stock	◑	◑	◑	◑	○	◑	○	○				◕				◕		2
Sylvie	Raw Stock			○			◕	◕	◕	◕			◕	○	◕	◑	◕		7
Teyjas	Raw Stock				◕	◔	◑	◕	◑	◑	◔	◔	◕	◑	◑		◑		3
Zhou	Raw Stock						◑		◑		◑	◑	◑	◕	◑	◔	◑		1
Sunil	Raw Stock				◕	◑	◑	◑			◕	◕	◕			○	◕		6
Chrissy	Raw Stock	○	○				○	○			○	○				○	○	○	0
																			0
Currently Capable (Levels 3 & 4)		1	2	2	3	1	2	2	2	2	1	1	6	2	2	1	4	0	0
Key	● = Level 4 (can instruct) ◕ = Level 3 (on own) ◑ = Level 2 (with supervision) ◔ = Level 1 (in training) ○ = Level 0 (needs to be trained)																		
	Shading indicates urgent need to ensure company capability																		

Figure 7.2 Trevor's training matrix filled out for the raw stock department.

I stumbled in my answer. "I want to get them trained."

"Interesting," said Julie. "That's not what you said two days ago." I did a double take.

"But that's what we talked about," I protested.

"Sure it is, among other things," she observed. "But it isn't what you eventually concluded your target was."

After a bit of discussion, I remembered what she was saying. I always wanted to be able to produce, even if one or two of my team were unavailable. I repeated it now.

"Yes," Julie noted. "Good. So with that in mind, let's look at your situation again. Given your target, you have some obstacles. Which one are you going to work on first?"

"I should probably start where I'm most at risk, I guess," I offered.

After a couple of minutes' discussion, we'd settled on the CNC. I had only one person, Sunil, who could reliably use it, and though we didn't use it more than a couple of hours a day, we needed it almost every day and every one of our products has at least one part made there. To top it off, it was an unusual machine – I wasn't aware of another one in the city. *It* was where I was most vulnerable.

"So your immediate obstacle is getting the people you need trained up on the CNC, right?" I nodded.

"What is the next step you can make to remove that obstacle? And what do you expect to learn?"

That wasn't the question I was expecting. Maybe, "Who should you train?" Maybe, "What do you need to train the person?" Maybe, "How soon can you have someone trained?" Not, "What is the next step?" I was confused.

Julie asked if I knew how to proceed, and I acknowledged that I didn't. "So, if you're not entirely sure how to proceed, the best we can do is to test out an idea, right? And then we can see if it makes the difference you're looking for."

Julie pointed out that unless we're sure about a result, we're doing an experiment. She indicated that she'd rather be clear about when we're doing something we know will work, and when we're experimenting. Because how we deal with the situation is very different.

After a few minutes more conversation, I realized that my next experiment – my next step was to see if a training program for the CNC would address my need. But since I didn't have one, I had another obstacle to deal with. So my next step was really to work out a training program. I figured that if

I spoke with Sunil we could figure out the things we needed to train someone so they could do most of the tasks solo.

"What do you expect to learn if you do that?" she asked. I must have looked lost. "Look, you're going to take some action. I'm sure you're taking it because you expect to be further ahead than you are now. You'll have learned something. What are you expecting to learn?"

Yikes. What a question. But as I thought about it, I realized that by the time I'd talked to Sunil, and maybe watched the operation for a day, I hoped I'd have learned what we need to teach someone to get them started on the CNC.

Then it suddenly occurred to me. "Wait a minute, Julie. I think there have been about four people who've tried to learn the CNC and they all failed. So I'm wondering…" I trailed off, not sure if I should voice my fear.

"What is it?" Julie asked?

"Well, I'm just wondering if Sunil really wants anyone to know how to use the CNC. He might think that being the only one gives him job security."

"True enough," she agreed. "But you know that machine, don't you?"

"Sure. But I know it because Dad had one like it in his workshop, and after he died, and Mum let me, I taught myself how to use every one of his machines. Had some close calls! But I figured them all out. Probably not beautiful to watch but I can do anything the machine can handle."

"So, could you watch someone we hired off the street and tell if they knew their way around the machine?"

"No problem. In my sleep."

"So he doesn't really have any job security, does he?" I shook my head. "Now I wouldn't suggest we go in and threaten him with no job security. That's not who Mrs. Kumar is, nor is it what she wants this company to be. Not who I want to be either. But we also can't be beholden to Sunil. So, would Sunil be a good person to learn the drill press?"

"Sure would. Super reliable. Doesn't make many mistakes. Careful." I carried on. "I see what you're thinking. We need him to learn the drill press, but to do that he has to be able to leave the CNC for a while. So someone else has to learn the CNC. And we could get him to teach whoever it is?" I mused.

"I don't think so," countered Julie.

I was surprised. He was the best operator. Shucks – he was the only operator. "What makes you say that?"

"Well, four things. First, he's a good operator, but my guess is he's had no more training in how to instruct than you have. Second, if four people have tried to learn from him and it hasn't worked, that's not very promising. Third, I need you to know this training stuff cold. You have to get it. And finally, I've been watching Sunil. He's bored. He needs something to challenge him, and working with you on this problem would do that very nicely."

"So I want the two of you to work together on the training for the CNC. And that means that the two of you and the others will learn how to train together."

My eyebrows went up.

"Don't be surprised," she went on. "I've got similar issues in the other departments. With five departments and two people from each, it will be the perfect-sized class. We're going to start next week. Tomorrow you and I will have a conversation with Sunil and put it to him."

The conversation happened next afternoon. I was surprised, but Sunil seemed genuinely excited that he was being asked to learn the drill press, and being asked to learn how to train people to use the CNC. It went way better than I'd expected.

The next week we did the five sessions of the Job Instruction program. It was strange to me, after five years with Rocky, to have my boss taking time to train us. It was a lot of fun and we kept shaking our heads as we thought about the way we'd been training up 'til then. We learned the Training Within Industry four-step method for instruction. I really liked the Job Instruction card that Julie gave to each of us, and it made things way easier for me to remember (Figure 7.3).

The method was surprising to me, how it broke the job down into steps, and how it separated out the important steps, the key points and the reasons. The hardest part for me to get consistently right when doing the breakdown was not to turn key points about how to do a step into a step itself. I also found it tricky to figure out just how much to include in each JI breakdown. Julie told us that getting the size right was a matter of trial and error – how much could people easily learn. She also reassured me that the method was robust enough that even if we didn't do it perfectly, it would still help the learners a lot. Still it felt pretty shaky. Later, I got better at both those bits.

Sunil took to it well. We were really excited two weeks later when we had picked Teyjas to learn the CNC. We did the first lesson about how to run simple parts though the CNC. Teyjas did a great job, and we came away thinking that we were going to be able to get this.

Sussex Creek
BOATWORKS

JOB INSTRUCTION

STEP 1 – PREPARE THE WORKER

1. Put the person **AT EASE**
2. State the **JOB**
3. Find out what the person **ALREADY KNOWS**
4. Get the person **INTERESTED** in learning the Job
5. Place the person in the correct **POSITION**

STEP 2 – PRESENT THE OPERATION

1. **SHOW** the operation
2. Tell, show **IMPORTANT STEPS,** one at a time.
3. Do it again, stressing **KEY POINTS**
4. Do it again, stating **REASONS** for key points

Instruct clearly, completely and patiently; don't give them more than they can master at once.

STEP 3 – TRY OUT PERFORMANCE

1. Have the person **DO THE JOB**; correct errors
2. Have the person explain each **IMPORTANT STEP** as they do the job again
3. Have the person explain each **KEY POINT** as they do the job again
4. Have the person explain the **REASONS** for each Key Point as they do the job again

Make sure the person understands.
Continue until YOU know THEY know.

STEP 4 – FOLLOW UP

1. Put the person **ON THEIR OWN**
2. Designate **WHO** the person goes to for **HELP**
3. Check on the person **FREQUENTLY**
4. Encourage **QUESTIONS**
5. **TAPER OFF** extra coaching and close follow up

IF THE WORKER HASN'T LEARNED,
THE INSTRUCTOR HASN'T TAUGHT.

Sussex Creek
BOATWORKS

JOB INSTRUCTION

HOW TO GET READY TO INSTRUCT

1. **Make a Time Table for Training**
   Who to train...
       For which work...
           By what date...
   Use the Job Training Matrix

2. **Break Down the Job**
   List **IMPORTANT STEPS**
     Answers "What do I do next?"
     Logical advance of the work
     Something is transformed
     Maximum 8
   Select **KEY POINTS**
     Answers "How do I do it correctly?"
     Safety matters are always Key Points
     Tips or Tricks
     Knack
     Tolerances
   State **REASONS**
     Answers "Why do it this way?"
     Law or policy
     Consequence when you don't do the step correctly

3. **Get Everything Ready**
   The proper equipment, tools, materials and whatever else is required to aid instruction

4. **Arrange the Worksite**
   Neatly, as in actual working conditions

Figure 7.3   The TWI Job Instruction card Julie created for Sussex Creek Boatworks.

Our Job Instruction Breakdown (Figure 7.4) sure helped us with the training process. And Teyjas found it helpful afterwards as a reminder. But Julie had been insistent that we had to do the training first *before* we showed Teyjas the Job Instruction breakdown.

COMPANY	Sussex Creek Boatworks	Page 1 of 1

Job Instructions for:	**Operate CNC Machine**
Parts Required:	Wood Blanks Sized as Noted on Work Order
Tools & Materials	See CNC Tool List on Work Order, Hex keys per shadow board, clean rags, plastic scoop, calipers
Date:	Issued Apr 21, 2019

Why This is Important Consequences to company and/or customers when the job not done right	If not operated correctly, parts will not fit, which will jeopardize shipping dates and add cost to re-make them.

Important Steps in the Operation	Key Points	Reasons
A logical segment of the operation when something happens to **advance** the work	Anything in the step that might - • injure the worker or others • "make or break" the job • make the work easier to do (i.e. "knack", "trick")	Reasons for the key Points (consequences if not done correctly)
1) Prep machine for part	• Verify tools in carousel match work order: When don't match call lead • Wipe spindle and chuck, vacuum chuck • Zero-touch first tool • Tighten adjustment nuts with hex key	• Correct tool used for each cut • Ensures tools sit correctly • Ensure dimensions match • Machine stays aligned
2) Enter part number	• Enter number twice	• Required. Reduces errors
3) Load wood blanks	• 1/8" clearance • MAX line visible	• Blanks will not jam • Top blank stays in place
4) Press start	• Close door • Trim parts from previous job during run • Listen for changes in sound – clear broken pieces as required, reload carrier and press start • Prepare next blanks	• Prevents chips from creating trip hazard • Prevents waste time • Warning that wood has broken – keeps machine running • Reduces machine idle time
5) Remove machined parts	• Check first part for critical dimensions – call supervisor when out of spec • Place parts in trim staging bin • Empty chips when MAX line not visible • Use plastic scoop • Reload carrier and go to Step 4 – repeat until count matches work order	• So guarantee parts fit together • Easy to reach for trimming • Chips don't hinder cutting • Plastic prevents machine damage • Reduces machine idle time
6) Clean machine	• After last part is correct • Remove all chips • Reset tool set to standard configuration • Vacuum machining chamber from top down	• Work order is complete • Clean for next run • Simplifies most set-ups • Minimizes dust

Figure 7.4   Trevor and Sunil's job breakdown for operating the CNC machine.

"If you give it to a learner before they've been through the task a few times, they don't listen. We can't afford to have that. Anyway, the right place for those documents is where the work gets done, not in the hands of individuals."[1]

What surprised me was the value of the repetition.[2] I'd known in some vague way that repetition helped with learning. But when I watched Teyjas learn I was amazed at the impact. First we did four demonstrations, adding more information each time. Then, he started doing it himself. It actually took six tries before we were ready to let him go on his own for a few minutes. But afterwards, Sunil was as certain as me that Teyjas was going to make the parts correctly.

It was a huge win for us.

Two days later, Julie came to watch as we taught Teyjas the first portion of the set-up process – how to take the previous tooling apart and put it away. It was the first time I'd ever seen someone trained how to take a set-up apart. But Teyjas did it very well by the end of the session. We saw him trying to tighten one bolt, rather than loosen it and corrected it immediately, gave him a tip about how to do it correctly, and from then on, he got it right. And I was excited that he would probably treat the tooling well enough that it would last longer – I was getting tired of dealing with nicks and scratches because people had been careless putting the tooling away.

After the session, Julie asked us how we thought the training was going.

"Pretty well," I said, "although it sure takes some time to get ready to do the training. I hadn't realized there were so many steps to sort through."

"Yup," she agreed. "There are. And you can just imagine that if there are that many steps, it is really easy for the learner to get it wrong if it isn't well laid out. You can also imagine that if you try to teach too much at once, the learner can get lost pretty easily." She went on to emphasize how critical it was to do the preparation work ahead of time, and set what gets included in a chunk based on some trials.

"Any other thoughts about today?" she asked.

Neither Sunil nor I had anything to say.

---

[1] Later she explained that the last thing we want is people stashing away personal copies of a Job Instruction Breakdown. Once it's out there it doesn't get updated, and then people wind up using non-standard methods. When it is kept by the machine, then it can be kept current.

[2] People typically need 8 to 10 repetitions to get to about 80% of peak performance, as long as all the repetitions are successful. See *https://bit.ly/3bpVOOX*. Research shows that for many tasks, people need 8–10 successful repetitions to reach about 80% of long-term performance.

Julie pointed out that as we had walked Teyjas through the steps we hadn't specifically numbered each step. Nor had we insisted that he number the steps as he did them. We just used, "the next step is…" and then "the next step is…" and on and on. So it was hard to keep track where we were.

Teyjas was over at his workstation.

"Go ask him how many important steps are in the operation he learned two days ago, and how many in today's session," Julie directed.

We went over and asked him. "For running the parts – that's easy. There were six. But I'm not sure about the set-up. It was way more confusing for me today. I'm not sure why." He went back to his task.

Sunil and I walked back to Julie. "What did you learn?" she asked.

"He knew there were six steps to run the machine, but didn't know how many steps there were in the put-away process."

"That's what you heard. What did you learn?" Curious – she didn't even seem to care what Teyjas's answer was!

I was stumped. I didn't understand her question. I felt like a fish out of water with its mouth opening and closing but nothing happening. Julie saw it.

"Look," she said, "you've reported what he said, and that's useful, but you need to make sense of that new information. What does it mean for your training activities? What conclusions can you draw from what you have heard?"

"Oh." I felt a bit chastened. She must have heard it in my voice.

"I know you haven't been pushed in this way before. You both have the ability to be good trainers. But to be great, you need to convert what you observe into new learning… So, what did you learn?"

"Well, when we stated the number of each step, then Teyjas remembered it and remembered how many steps there were. But when we didn't do that consistently, he didn't. So numbering seems to make a difference for the person learning."

"Well done," Julie exclaimed. "From a sample of one, you've drawn a very interesting conclusion. What I can do is help you along, because in the hundreds of times I've instructed using this method, your observation is true. So it isn't a sample of one… it is a sample of hundreds. Now you can take that lesson and adjust how you instruct. Of course, it's not that the numbering makes the memorizing easier – it's more like it provides a scaffold for the things he has to remember."

Sunil, usually very quiet, piped up. "I'm surprised how much the learners need things broken down. It seems that if we don't do that for them, it's much harder to learn."

"Another good lesson," Julie responded. "I'm sure you'll remember both of them when you do training in the future. What action can you take to make sure you don't forget?"

I didn't have any bright ideas and stayed silent. Sunil was silent, too, but that was pretty normal.

Julie didn't let us off the hook. "You each need to come up with at least five ideas of concrete steps you could take that ensure you do what you've learned. Then you need to pick one. I can wait here until you've finished."

I couldn't believe how patient Julie seemed – she just waited – not showing any anxiety or needing to be somewhere else. But she was sure making the point that this was important.

Four minutes later I had my five ideas. Sunil's ideas were pretty similar. My list was:

1. Block ½ hour into my calendar at least 1 hour before the training time
2. Make a checklist for training and include the preparation time
3. Put a note on my Job Instruction card
4. Review my training card with someone else before I do the training
5. Put a note in my phone

"So," Julie started, "what you have here are five hypotheses or guesses about what might work. The basic hypothesis is that if you do this action, you will better remember to number the important steps as you deliver the instruction. Which of these five ideas seems most promising at achieving that outcome?"

After some discussion, I concluded my best option – at least to start – was to put a note on my Job Instruction card. If it worked over the next three weeks, then I could treat that problem as solved. If not, I'd have to try something else.

As it turned out, the note on my Job Instruction card worked perfectly. I used it every time I did instruction, so I always looked at the note, and I never missed my prep time.

The next week Julie caught me after the morning meeting. "Do you have 10 minutes right now?" I did.

"Good," she went on. "I think I've found someone for you. I just finished my interview and I think she will fit. But she'll be on your team, so you need to speak to her. I need you to do two things for me, please. First, ask her enough questions that you are comfortable that she's not B.S.ing about what she knows about machining wood. Second, I want you to ask her enough questions about the problems she's solved that you are comfortable that she's not scared off by problems, and that she's got a we-can-fix-this attitude. Do you think you can do that?"

"Sure," I responded. "No problem."

"Then, just so I know I've explained it right, can you tell me the two things?"

"Yup. You want to know if she's bluffing about what she knows technically, and whether she'll fit in."

"Not quite," said Julie. "The first part's right. But the second one isn't just whether she'll fit in. It's whether, when she comes across a problem, she won't either freeze or try to pass off the responsibility for finding a solution. So we want to know how she's reacted to problems she's already encountered. Can you try that last one again?"

I guess I gave Julie enough comfort that she led me to the conference room and introduced me to Chrissy. She sure wasn't what I'd expect for a machinist – a tiny woman with a rich alto voice that for me didn't match the tiny stature of the person that produced it. Dressed very well, not like a shop person. It turns out she was on her way to her job as an executive assistant, but she hated being in an office. The interview went well. We got talking about cut angles and tool steel hardness, and she told me some really interesting things about one of our tool suppliers. In 10 minutes I was done.

I went to find Julie. "I'm through," I said. "I'd love to see her come in and spend a couple of hours showing us what she can do, but everything I heard sounded perfect. Where did you find her?"

"Best source I have," Julie replied. "My network. I put it out there that we were looking for someone, and Chrissy is the daughter of a neighbour of a former colleague. The neighbour is a woodworking nut, and apparently Chrissy just hung out with her dad forever. By the time she was ten she could use every tool in his shop. He made special stools so she'd be at the right height to run each one! I'll see when she can come in later this week, and how soon she can start. You or Sunil will need to train her, too, so have the Job Instruction Breakdown Sheets that you need to train her all ready. I figure she'll be here in two weeks."

***

The next week Julie asked me how the training was going. I was elated. Teyjas was turning into a very competent CNC operator. He had produced almost all the parts we made on the machine and was producing at the rate we expected for an experienced person. Sunil was excited that he could train so well, and was looking forward to learning the drill press. We had prepared and tried out about half of the 15 breakdowns we'd need for Chrissy's training. She'd be starting next week, and Sunil was lined up to spend about half his time after Monday morning training her. Between having Teyjas, Chrissy and Sunil trained on the CNC, we were going to meet my objective – at least for that machine.

Julie smiled. "You've done well, Trevor. Learning to instruct effectively is such a critical skill for any supervisor. Are you having fun with it?"

"Sure am," I replied. "It's so much fun to see people able to perform new skills and see their face light up when they realize they can do it."

"I'm right with you on that," Julie commented. "I'm glad you see it that way. So if you're open to it, I'd like you to keep on doing training and eventually you can start training people how to train. If you're interested, I need you to make time to teach at least another ten skills over the next three months. Basically one a week. If you can get that done, then we can see about the next step."

I went home that night almost dancing. I phoned my sister and talked her ear off.

***

The following week Sunil and I started to develop the training program for the drill press. He didn't know how to use it, but he'd been through the how-to-train class with me, and I figured if he helped me write the Job Instruction Breakdowns and then was trained by me, he'd have a very good grasp of the drill press. It worked out super well. We got Sylvie involved and Jas a bit too, and discovered that they did some things differently. So we got them to agree on how they would both do it. By now that part was coming easier for both Sunil and me. Ask each of them what they did, compare the two, then bring them together and ask about the differences: what was each of them trying to achieve with those differences. Usually they could see that one way was better, and when we couldn't, we'd ask about the rate of problems at that step. Then it would be pretty clear. By the time we had the Job Instruction Breakdowns done, we were seeing the production rate go up!

The training for Chrissy went well. She turned out to be a great addition to the team. She was so tiny that we made a platform for her that she could roll around to wherever she was working! But by the end of the first week she was producing like she'd been there for months, and it seemed that she couldn't be happier being surrounded by wood and sawdust.

On a whim, at the end of her first week, I asked Julie if we could give her a boat to take home, as a "you got through the first week" thank you. Julie loved the idea. I got one of the guys in the finishing department to laser etch Chrissy's initials across the stern before the finish was applied. To this day we give a brand-new customized boat to every employee at the end of their first week! It also launched a new service, because we started offering that etching to our customers. It was really well received and added a lot to our profit from each boat.

In between Sunil's time with Chrissy and some production work of his own, I started training him the week after Chrissy started. For Sunil it was the manual practice that mattered, since he knew the content. By the end of 40 minutes he was producing at the rate we'd expect for an experienced operator!

By the end of the week, just eight weeks after Steve left, Sunil and I had learned to train, we had Teyjas and Chrissy running the CNC well, Sunil was on his way to learning the drill press, Sylvie and Jas had both improved their production rate, and I was feeling like I'd met my objective.

I turned my attention to the other gaps on my training matrix.

***

A month later I caught Julie at the end of a production meeting and I walked beside her as she headed out to the plant.

"You know the training matrix you had me do when we had that problem with Steve leaving?" The problem was long resolved, but we both remembered the work we'd had to do to get those orders out. Julie nodded and smiled.

"Well you said that if I had some ideas about the matrix I should come to you after I'd used it the way it was for two months. Two months is up, and I have an idea."

Julie stopped walking. "This is great," she stated. "Show me!" Her eyes lit up.

"Well, I kept having people coming up to me asking how many people we needed capable of each task. I kept having to figure out how many at each level for each task, and I had to keep track of it. They wanted to know what to ask for training in.

"I realized that if I put a couple more rows at the bottom, I could show how many we needed for each task at the Competent and Trainer levels. So what if we do it like this." I showed her a printout (Figure 7.5).

Training Matrix for Sussex Creek Boatworks DATE YYYY/MM/DD

Task columns: Forklift, Receive Offcuts, Receive Goods, Planer, Planer - Change Blade, Jointer, Jointer - Change Blade, Chop Saw, Chop Saw - Change Bl, CNC Milling Machine Operate, CNC Milling Machine Set Up, Pallet Jack, Band Saw, Finger Jointer, Drill Press, Read Work Order, TOTAL CAPABILITY, Individual Targets (not published)

Procedure or work instruction reference - if none indicate: None (across all task columns)

Name	Job Description and reference	Now	Q1	Q2	Q2
Marcus	Raw Stock	8		1	
Jas	Raw Stock	7			
Giles	Raw Stock	2	2	4	
Sylvie	Raw Stock	7			
Teyjas	Raw Stock	3	1	2	
Zhou	Raw Stock	1		2	
Sunil	Raw Stock	6	1		
Chrissy	Raw Stock	0	4	2	
		0			

Currently Capable (Levels 3 & 4): 1 2 2 3 1 2 2 2 2 1 1 6 2 2 1 4 0 0

Targets:
- End Q1: 2 2 2 4 1 3 3 2 2 3 3 6 2 2 3 4 — Individual target 8
- End Q2: 2 3 3 4 2 3 3 3 2 3 3 6 3 4 3 7 — Individual target 11
- End Q3: (blank)
- End Q4: (blank)

Key:
- ● = Level 4 (can instruct)
- ◑ = Level 3 (on own)
- ◔ = Level 2 (with supervision)
- ◕ = Level 1 (in training)
- ○ = Level 0 (needs to be trained)

Shading Indicates urgent need to ensure company capability

Figure 7.5 Trevor's suggestion for an extended training matrix.

"One other thing, too. If I put these columns on the right, then I can see how many skills each person has, and I can go to them and nudge them to improve their skill sets. I think that would really help us with people like Zhou. My hypothesis is that if they see their total in comparison to others, they may want to improve."

Her eyes moved over the page. "I think you've come up with a really interesting improvement. Are there any obstacles you're aware of?"

"Nope. Just need your OK."

"How does this help you with your target, and what do you expect to learn from this experiment?"

I knew those questions were coming. I was ready. "My hypothesis is that if I show people where the needs are, I'll get more people asking for training in just the areas where we're short, so it won't make a difference to production if somebody is sick or away. And I think if I put this up and people see it, I'll probably get a response from my team members within a week."

"OK. I see one thing that you might want to think about. If you are Zhou, might you be a bit embarrassed by this?"

"Maybe," I admitted.

"So, before you post this publicly, you might want to show this to Zhou and Giles and Teyjas, and, if they want, see if you can get them competent in a couple more skills before it gets posted. Then they can look better."

"Apart from that," Julie finished up, "it makes sense to me. Go for it." She turned off to another part of the plant. Then she turned back to me. "Oh, Trevor. Good work. That's a great idea to try. I want to hear how it goes." And then she was off.

Two weeks later I was able to report that my "experiment" was a success. Zhou and Giles had both expressed interest in learning new skills and had done so, so their rows showed a wider skill set. Teyjas was still learning the CNC, and decided that it was enough for now. There were people who wanted training in every one of the areas where we were a bit short.

Now my challenge was to get everyone trained before we needed the new skills. With my training matrix in hand I had a solid handle on where I needed to start.

Reflecting on the Chapter

For Supervisors

- What skill shortages have you run into in your area? What were the last three situations where you couldn't deliver because you didn't have enough people with the right skills? Had you seen that problem before, or was it new?
- How do you currently keep track of the skills of each member of your team?
- When did you last do training in your area? How did you do it? How did you know that the learner was good enough to be put on his or her own?
- What portion of the mistakes in your area can be attributed to unreliable skills?
- The last few times you trained someone, how many repetitions were there before you set the person on their own?

Actions to Take

- Prepare a skill matrix for your team. Identify how many people you need with each skill. You can download a blank skill matrix form at www.becomingthesupervisor.com/downloads.
- For the next training you need to do, prepare by organizing the information you will present into the important steps, key points and reasons. See how that changes your instruction. Assess whether it helped the learner. You can download a blank Job Instruction Breakdown Sheet at http://www.becomingthesupervisor.com/downloads. Also see the Techniques for Better Performance section at the end of this chapter.

For Managers (you have supervisors reporting to you)

Consider all the questions for supervisors for yourself. Then consider the following.

- What support do your supervisors need to learn how to instruct more effectively?
- Is any of your production being limited because of how long it takes to train people? If so, what is it about the training that makes it take so long?

- Which of your supervisors is more effective in getting their people up to speed? What are they doing that results in that difference? What can you do to help your other supervisors try the same approach?

Actions to Take

- Observe each of your supervisors the next time they train someone. Do not interrupt or take over – just observe. If you need to do correction, take the supervisor aside after (unless what they're teaching creates a safety hazard). Watch and listen for important steps, key points and reasons. How many repetitions do the learners have before they are set on their own?
- Read the article **Why Standard Work is not Standard: Training Within Industry Provides an Answer** by Jim Huntzinger (*Target*, Vol. 22, No. 4, 2006, pp. 7–13) (http://twisummit.com/standard/). It provides a useful overview of how good instruction can help you establish standard work – the current best way to do a task.
- Help each of your supervisors develop a skill matrix for their team. Guide them as they train people for the skills that pose the greatest risk to sustained production.

Techniques for Better Performance

Prepare Job Instruction Breakdown Sheets

This instruction will help you prepare concise Job Instruction Breakdown Sheets that you can use to deliver instruction. Doing this, and using it to guide your instruction will make it clearer and faster. You can download a blank Job Instruction Breakdown Sheet at www.becomingthesupervisor. com/downloads.

This approach will help you break down each job into teachable units. You can also use the Job Instruction breakdown sheet as an auditing tool, to check whether a worker is doing the job according to the best currently known method.

As you start using this, focus on tasks where you are having quality issues, or where it takes a long time for people to learn the task, or where you cannot produce enough.

You can use this for physical tasks, as in a manufacturing plant, as well as in clerical and administrative tasks (accounting, financial analysis, HR, sales, IT) and even for more complex tasks like sales or research.

Important Step	Key Points	Reasons
A logical segment of the operation when something happens to advance the work	Highlights aspects of how to do the task: methods that might • "make or break" the job • injure the worker or others • make the work easier to do (i.e. "knack," "trick," special timing, or a bit of special information)	Reasons for the key points
1. Write Important Steps	• Must advance the work • Answers the question "What do I do next?" • Maximum 8 • Complete important steps before writing key points or reasons	• Easier to remember • Easier to remember • Easier to remember • Helps get sequence right

(Continued)

Important Step	*Key Points*	*Reasons*

2. Develop Key Points	• Four types
	  • "Make or break" elements
	
	  • Safety issues related to the procedure
	  • Tips, tricks, or knacks
	  • Tolerances important for the step
	• Answers the question "*How should I do it?*"
	
	• Use "When" statements for conditional operations: "When X condition exists, do Y"
	• Phrase all points in the positive
		• Prevents serious errors
		• Reduces risk of accidents
		• Easier to do
		• Avoid unneeded effort
		• Distinguish Important Steps from Key Points
		• "When" is directive: always do it this way when condition exists
		• Keeps focus on how to do it right, away from all the possible errors

3. Provide Reasons	• Describe the consequences if key points are not observed • At least one reason for each key point • Rarely requires theory • Legal or policy requirements	• Makes the importance of key points clear • The key point has to matter to the result or it should be ignored • Theory rarely helps understand the task or consequences • Know that it is the law

(*Continued*)

Important Step	Key Points	Reasons
4. Document the results	• Use the company's standard form • Use ~~as~~ few words ~~as possible~~ • Pencil OK	• Consistent format makes it easier for others to train • A reminder, not instruction • Better to have hand-written than not available
5. File the completed form	• Use company practice for filing • Scan handwritten forms • Store electronic copies in a widely available location	• Others can find it easily • Makes it available faster • So it is always available

Chapter 8

The New Order – Making Improvements

The next several weeks were the best of summer – long hot days and nights cool enough to sleep comfortably. By common consent at this time of year, the whole plant started and ended the workday an hour earlier. Most of us were away by two, which gave us most of the afternoon to take advantage of the weather. It also meant that we didn't have to work through the heat of the day.

There were a couple of people who stayed more regular hours to answer the phones during conventional business hours, but they wanted to be there, and they were happy to stay in the air-conditioned office.

The weeks seemed to carry on in an endless parade of glorious days.

On the Monday, four weeks into this wonderful stretch of weather, Julie came into our daily stand-up meeting. She was almost bouncing. The grin on her face announced her excitement, and I could see the team looking around at each other with questions in their eyes.

We started through the agenda of the stand-up meeting. By now it was routine. I'd heard a couple of my colleagues comment that they'd never been to meetings that were useful before. Then we got to the point at the end of the meeting where new stuff was brought up.

Julie's grin just got bigger. "I was telling my boss at my last company what we're doing," she started.

"Just working on an escape clause in case you can't fix us?" gibed Gil.

Julie didn't miss a beat. "Nope. Working on your escape clause." Gil reddened. "I think most of you know that my last company made large agricultural equipment. Each piece ran $250,000 to $500,000, and I once saw a special order go through the plant that was almost $700,000. That's a lot of money, and my former boss wants a tangible and different way to say thank you to their customers. He's thinking about giving each customer of the bigger machines a couple of our boats as a gift. You know, a fleet for the farmer's children or grandchildren. For the smaller units, customers would just get one. He wants their company logo laser etched on the funnel of each boat. They sell a thousand to twelve hundred units a year, so we're talking about an order for fifteen or sixteen hundred boats. That's a lot."

"There has to be a catch," Gil muttered.

"Of course there is," Julie retorted as she smiled. "We normally sell these boats at about $82, and we have costs of $50. That gives us a gross margin of 39% – not great but tolerable for the moment. He can't justify paying more than $68. Even at that price his order would be over $100,000 a year. And if he's giving us that much business, all at once, we can afford to drop our gross margin by 7%–8% for his orders, since we have virtually no selling costs. Still, and this is the catch, to make this order work, we have to get our costs down from $50 to $42 or $43. Of course, if we can do that, our margins will go up on everything, which will help our profitability, and the bonuses you'll get. Back to your retirement, Gil.

"I told him I need a week to figure out if we can get to his target price. What I need from you folks is a way to make this happen. How can we change our production process to take 15% out of the cost? Can you put your heads together and give me your first thoughts tomorrow?"

I should have recognized the signs. But so should Julie. She should have picked up on what was going on. I guess she's not perfect yet, either. No-one volunteered. There was a general nodding of heads, but no-one stepped up and said they'd drive it. It was just left hanging.

I know I was thinking that I didn't have a clue how to start. I certainly didn't see anyone standing around for 15% of the day. And we'd started to see our scrap levels drop, so that wasn't going to get us much. I just didn't have a clue. I don't think the others did, either. So none of us stepped up.

Of course, the next day, when Julie asked about our progress at the stand-up meeting, there were mumbles all around about "didn't get to it," and "no ideas here." Julie looked around. There was some disappointment on her face. But she had that far-away look that I was recognizing more often. She snapped out of it. "Right. I want everyone, no exceptions, at a meeting tomorrow at one in the boardroom. You don't need to do anything before then. Just have the work for your teams lined up so you won't be interrupted during the last hour of the day."

Wednesday went OK as a production day. No big issues. No drama. It was nice. And all through the day I kept looking around trying to see where I could cut costs by 15%. I was also nervous because the only times I'd heard about cost cutting the discussion was always followed by layoffs. I didn't want to be laying anyone off, especially since we'd just got Chrissy on board and trained.

Just before one we all trooped into the boardroom. We were sure grateful for the air conditioning. It was a blistering day; the plant was uncomfortably hot.

Julie rushed in. She put her stuff down, settled herself, and looked around at us all. It was really uncanny how in three seconds she seemed to be able to look each of us in the eye and pull us into her orbit. It was only a year later that Julie coached me to be able to do that. I still don't know many people who can, though it is learnable.

"I need to start with an apology," she began quietly. I could see the questioning looks around the room. "I set you a task that you're not ready for, and didn't take time to think through what I was asking. I put you in a position where you couldn't succeed. That's not a boss's job, and I messed up. I'm sorry, and I'll try to do better.

"I've done some thinking about why that happened. I can see several things that contributed to it, but it's still my fault for not getting this right. I was really excited about the potential for the order. The place I used to work, we were five years into this process, and so almost everyone on the team had all the basic skills. I forgot that you are all just starting out on this journey towards continuous improvement. I hope you'll forgive me.

"I've thought about a countermeasure. I need you to tell me when what I'm asking is new to you. That's it. If it's new to you, let me know. That can be a useful trigger to me to rethink how we do something, and I won't leave you hanging out to dry. Is everyone OK with that?"

There was silence for a few moments.

Terri from shipping responded. "It's OK, Julie. I get it. I can do that. This feels really awkward. Rocky would have just screamed at us and this feels really weird in comparison."

There were several breaths let out. And then voices around the room saying "thank you."

The room seemed to relax.

"Thanks for accepting my apology," Julie said. She paused a moment. "Are we OK to go after our challenge now?"

Heads nodded around the table.

Julie stepped up to the whiteboard. She started by asking us to describe the entire process from start to finish. As we did so, she wrote it on the whiteboard as a sort of block diagram. She was using some symbols I didn't understand, but I could see the sweep of our production laid out on the board. A couple of times she would draw it wrong, but seemed just fine when one of us corrected her.

"Does this pretty much show our process?" she asked.

Again, heads nodded around the table.

"OK. Tell me, what are the most expensive steps – either because it takes so much time from people, or because it's hard to get right, or it just is, and we're not really sure why."

After a bit of discussion, we identified three areas where we knew it cost us a lot. One was my area – parts production. The others were rough finishing, and, surprisingly, packaging. I'd always figured the packaging was dead simple – a bit of foam, wrap the boat and stick it in a box. But apparently it cost a lot of money to do it. The things you learn!

Julie's next question came out of left field. "How could we eliminate these steps?"

"What do you mean, eliminate?" I countered. "You can't make boats without parts. And you can't ship them without packing them."

"I suppose not," she replied, "but maybe we can eliminate parts of what we do. For example, if we look at rough finishing, what's the purpose of rough finishing? What is it for?"

"We have to make the boats smooth enough that we can do the finish sanding quickly. If we don't do the rough finishing it would take hours to get the boats to the finished dimensions with the fine sandpaper. And we have to do fine sanding so it looks great when we put the finish on it."

"But why aren't the boats smooth enough when we put them together?" Julie questioned.

"Well, actually, they are smooth enough…they're just oversize," commented Peter.

"What's the purpose of them being oversize?" inquired Julie.

"We machine them to be a bit big so that if the gluing isn't perfect, we can sand down the edges to make the parts match."

"So if we could line up the pieces perfectly every time we could eliminate rough finishing?" Julie was pushing us.

"I suppose," acknowledged Peter. "But I can't imagine how we'd do that. The parts often slip a bit as we clamp them, and we don't want to clamp from the side because then the glue sticks to the clamp and it gets hard to unclamp them. Also, if there is glue that squeezes out it affects how the wood absorbs the finishes, so we have to sand that glue line. Also, our clamps are straight, so we really can't get them lined up perfectly. There'd be a twist as often as not."

"Any other thoughts?," Julie persisted. "I've heard you describe three different obstacles. Julie got up and wrote on the whiteboard.

1. Parts slip
2. Glue-free surface
3. Clamps are straight

"Let me see if I have this right," she started. "The parts slip when we clamp them with the wet glue. We need to have a glue-free surface for the finish. And, we don't have curved clamps that could keep the parts in line."

"And so, because we can't control these, we machine the parts oversize so we can sand them down to overcome these issues. Are there any other obstacles to eliminating the rough sanding?"

There was silence for 30 seconds.

"If you could just remove one of those obstacles, which would make the biggest difference, do you think?"

Peter started. "I guess that if we could stop the parts from slipping, then we could reduce the amount of oversize allowance. It might not eliminate the rough sanding, but it sure would reduce it and make it way faster. And if they didn't slip, then the clamp issue wouldn't matter. So my vote is try to stop the slipping."

"Hmmm." Julie was clearly mulling something over. "Have any of you ever seen an application where the position of parts is guaranteed?"

"What about IKEA furniture?" Jas suggested. "They just have flat pieces, and they guarantee the position by using those dowels."

"Say, I've seen something like that in my sewing," said Farah. "They do little diamond points wherever the two pieces of fabric are supposed to meet."

"And my kid's plastic models have little pins that force the plastic parts to line up perfectly," offered Art. "It's actually pretty much like our situation, because they don't want glue showing either."

"Is there a way we can use one of those ideas for our situation?" Julie asked.

"What if we machined a little bump into the edges at particular spots, and little holes into the mating spot?" asked Farah.

"What would it take to try that out?" Julie asked.

I chimed in. "We'd need to get Alex to change the program for each mating joint. If we were just doing a trial it would probably take him an hour or so. And we might need a slightly different starting size for the part. So maybe a couple of hours to set up the machining program, and then an hour at most to machine half a dozen sets and try them out."

Julie looked around at us. "Wan'na try an experiment?" she grinned. No one said anything. "I'm not hearing any objections?" she questioned after a very long pause.

"OK, Trevor. Make it happen. Can you have it done for tomorrow?"

"Not sure about that," I responded. "I don't know how much Alex has on his plate, and he's the only one who can do that stuff."

"Only one who can, or only one who's allowed," Julie shot back.

"Only one I know who can," I said.

"Well that's a problem," Julie commented. "For another time." She made a quick note in her book. "OK, Trevor. Can you make it happen for Monday?"

"Sure," I answered.

"Good. We'll see what we learn from this experiment. But that's not all," she said. We were each asked to list all the steps in the three expensive processes – parts production, rough sanding, and packaging. Anyone who didn't have one of these areas to look after was assigned to one of the three. Our task was to create the list of steps together for the next day. Farah was paired with me. She is in charge of prototyping, so she was going to be out of her element. I don't think she even knew all the machines we use.

"Any other questions?" Julie was clearly starting to wind up the meeting.

"Just one for now," I spoke up. "Every time I've ever heard about companies taking costs out of products it seems to be tied to letting people go. If we can take all this cost out, what's going to happen to our people? I'm not going to be very excited about it if all our efforts just put people out of work. And they're sure not going to contribute. I mean, why would they?"

I could see everyone around the room looking at me. The room was still.

"It's a really, really good question, Trev," she started. "When I was talking to Mrs. K before I joined Sussex Creek, I asked her the same question. You see I knew that to do my job I'd have to find ways to reduce the labour content of the boats, so I knew from the outset that this question would come up. Her view – what she said to me – is that we will not lay people off because they've found better ways to make the products. She saw her job as growing the sales side so that everyone keeps their job – and maybe we can even hire more people."

"Do you remember when I started, some of you asked if I was going to bring in automation? And we have, haven't we. Little bits here and there. We have another milling machine for our parts area, and it has simplified the work and reduced our costs. But our staff numbers haven't gone down because we're making more boats and we need everyone we have. I see the same thing continuing. If we get our costs down like we're trying to, the company will make more money, it will show up in our bonuses, and we'll all be able to go home on time every day. But no-one will lose their job."

As the meeting wound up, I lined up a time with Farah to spend an hour walking through the parts production area with her, so we could make the list Julie had asked for.

As we left the room, Gil caught my eye. He edged over to me as we walked down the hall. "Pretty gutsy to ask that," he muttered.

"Someone had to."

"Still, thanks. We were all thinking it," he commented. "I guess I'll believe it when I see it."

Next day at the stand-up meeting in my area, I mentioned the new opportunity and the challenge that we had, and the effort to take costs out of the parts production process. I made sure they knew we weren't singled out.

There were no answers during the meeting, but I guess the seed was planted. Half an hour later I walked by Teyjas as he was head down on an order. "Hey, Trevor," he called. I walked over. "Are you serious about trying to cut costs?" I nodded. "Then stop having us waste time."

"What do you mean?" I asked.

Teyjas launched into a list of things he thought were silly or a waste of his time.

- He spent 15 minutes a day looking for small tools that had gone astray.
- He ran into issues on the work orders at least twice a day that he would need to clarify with me – it cost him another 15 minutes.
- At least once a day he was looking for the designated raw material and then getting the forklift to bring it over to his workstation – another 15 minutes.

There were others. By the time he finished he had accounted for over an hour of his time that was spent not producing. And while some of the tasks had to be done, if he was doing them, it meant that the machines weren't running. As Rocky used to say, if we're not making sawdust, we're not making money. I'd learned from Julie that sometimes even when we were making sawdust, we were not making money, but it's still a pretty good reference point.

I thought back to when I was doing Teyjas' job three years before, and how all those details that slowed me down were so annoying. But eventually I just accepted them because that was how stuff was done, and Rocky never worried about it. Now, it seemed, we needed to worry about it.

Later that morning I met with Farah. I told her about my exchange with Teyjas and said that I thought that it might be helpful for us to make the list of the steps, but for each step, see what things could make it easier for the operators to do production – things like the items Teyjas had identified. We walked through the process and spoke to the operators.

At the breakdown saw, we talked to Zhou, who was working on a pallet of offcuts from one of our suppliers. We spoke to her about things that made it hard for her to do her job. We heard again about issues in the work orders and getting the right raw material at her workstation. Then her tone of voice changed. "May I tell you problem I have?"

"Of course," I replied, not sure what was coming.

"Mr. Trevor." She hesitated. She had called me Mr. Trevor from the day I was appointed as supervisor. I'd tried to have her drop the "Mr.," but she had insisted. "Mr. Trevor," she started again, "Lots of wood." She pointed at the tote of wood beside the saw. "All different sizes. Very slow. Every piece adjust saw. Many mistakes, then wood too short. Look here." She pointed to the waste bin. It was full of short off-cuts – not big enough to do anything with. "So much waste. Too much waste," she said.

"Let me get this straight," I said. "Because the wood comes in with so many sizes in a tote, you have to re-set the saw for every piece, and that makes it harder and slows you down. And sometimes then you don't set it quite right so you end up cutting off the wrong amount. Then you have to start over."

Zhou nodded. "Yes. Very often," clearly delighted that I had understood.

"Hmmm," I started. "How many times a day, do you think?" I needed to know how big an issue this was.

Zhou laughed. "Not times a day. Times an hour."

"Tell me then, if you run twenty pieces, would this problem happen to one or two of the pieces?"

"Not one. Not two. Maybe … five."

"So this happens to maybe one piece out of every four."

"Yes," she exclaimed. "Yes!" Her eyes smiled when she saw I understood. "One in four."

That *was* a problem. When I had done the breakdown job five years before, we had been getting longer pieces than we did now, so I could cut as many as half a dozen blanks out of each piece. But now, as I looked at the tote, most of the pieces were near our minimum. I realized that the job Zhou was doing was very different from the job I'd done. I could see that Zhou's task would be hard work and hard to get consistently right. It also sounded like opportunity, but I didn't know what that would look like.

I thanked Zhou. Then Farah and I continued our walk.

At the end of the hour, I shook my head. "Farah, it looks to me like all these little obstacles wind up costing each of our production people at least an hour every day. That's 15% more production right there, if we can find ways to eliminate all the obstacles. It will also make it easier for our staff – and make it easier to make the parts right. And that's not even looking at any other opportunities.

"I think there is a real opportunity to make Zhou's job easier and reduce our breakdown costs. If she had a more efficient method, we might cut her time in half. It's sure not the saw that's limiting her."

That afternoon Julie came by. I went over what Farah and I had found. She seemed very pleased. Then she asked which ones would make the most difference? I didn't know how to answer her.

"I think what we need to do is introduce you and a couple of the others to Job Methods – or at least part of it. It is a very good set of simple tools that can help you think through which ideas to do first. I'm going to be meeting with Arthur, Peter, and Farah about that late Monday morning. Can you make it?"

And I'm going to say "no" to my boss who wants to teach me something? Not a chance. However, I did check my calendar first. "Yup," I answered. "What time do you want me there?"

She gave me the time and we carried on.

"Do you think, given what you've seen, that we can get our unit costs down by 15%?"

I thought about it for a moment. Every one of my staff had found an hour or more that they saw as waste. And then I had a couple of situations like Zhou's, where I figured we could cut the time in half with some change to the way the work was done.

"Yeah," I started. "I don't think we can get it all done in a week. I don't even know if we can ever get *all* the improvements I saw put in place.

But give us a couple of months and I'm pretty sure we can get you 15%, and with a couple of small investments, it can probably go to 20%."

"That's good news," she said. "I'll give everyone an update at tomorrow's meeting."

Late in the day I had a few minutes and went to Farah's prototype shop. I loved that shop because it was so well equipped and so compact. It reminded me of my dad's shop in our basement.

I told her what I told Julie.

"That sounds pretty reasonable," she observed. "You know she's going to want to know when you're going to do it, don't you, whether we get that order or not. She's like my dad…too sharp a business person to let go of an opportunity like that to reduce her costs. And you know she's going to want us to use these ideas for every product, don't you?"

"You're probably right," I started.

"Probably?" she said tauntingly. "For sure. For certain, certain sure. I'll bet you a coffee and a muffin that regardless of her decision about the order, we will have to do this stuff."

"OK," I said weakly. I knew she was right.

As it turned out, Farah was exactly right.

At the end of the next day's stand-up meeting, Julie announced that she'd heard about enough opportunities to reduce our costs that she was going to take the order. "The great thing," she started, "is that we'll use these ideas for every product we sell, and we'll see our margins overall go up by 8 to 10%. I calculate that we're going to wind up with about three people who will be freed up for other activity if we don't bring in more orders. I'll be telling Mrs. K that we need to push up sales by 5% to 10% overall."

She looked around at us all. She had a grin on her face like a cat that has just caught a mouse. "I love it when production puts pressure on Sales to perform better." She looked directly at Yvonne – she heads our sales efforts. "You can expect some experiments in the next month or two on the sales side. Yvonne, are you paying attention?" We haven't seen much of her since Julie started; she's been on the road so much. She nodded back at Julie.

"We won't be making any changes in people until we've started to see some of the gains," she went on. "But I don't want this to catch any of us by surprise. By the end of next week I need you to have gone through your staff lists, and identified one or two people who are ready for a new challenge." She paused and looked around at each of us. Maybe glared would be a better word. "This is NOT an opportunity to get rid of your weakest people. The person I want is the one with the greatest potential. I also need you to have figured out who needs what training so that the person you've identified can leave your area without a hiccup."

By the end of the following week, we had all identified who would be freed up and figured out our training requirements. We decided that Sylvie would be the person from my team to participate. At the beginning of the next week Julie met with the three people we had picked to be freed up, together with their supervisors, so they all knew what was coming. Then, that afternoon we had a company meeting to let our staff know about this potential new customer and the implications it had. Mrs. K was there and stated her commitment to keep everyone on the team even as we improved our productivity. I don't know if it was her idea or Julie's but it was like the whole room relaxed when she said it... like we'd all been holding our breath and then, as one, let it out.

As we were getting ready to go home, I caught up with Farah. "You won that bet. When do you want to go for a coffee?"

Reflecting on the Chapter

For Supervisors

- What has your experience of improvement efforts been? Were people laid off, or rewarded? Think about the situation at your current company and at the last place you worked. What was the impact on staff of the events you observed?
- When you are being pushed to get stuff out, which is the problematic part of your area – what is it that you are always waiting for?
- Given what you know, do your customers care more about how long it takes to get delivery, how reliable the product or service is, or the cost of what you supply?
- If the production capacity in your area is not being pressed, how much more could you do with the people you have now?

Actions to Take

- Speak to each of the people on your team and ask what is causing them to lose time or making their work difficult. Find something you can do that improves their work.
- Walk through the process in your area. Identify which parts of the process require the most people time, regardless of the reason. Then observe the process at the operation that takes the most time, and see if you can identify an improvement that could reduce that time.
- Look at each production step in your area and ask yourself what you would need to do to eliminate that step. If you cannot eliminate the step, consider whether there is a portion of the step you could eliminate. Identify what would need to change.

For Managers *(you have supervisors reporting to you)*

Consider all the questions for supervisors for yourself. Then consider the following.

- What has the experience of your supervisors been in regards to improvement efforts? Have improvements led to layoffs or rewards?

■ Which of your supervisors has been able to increase the output of their area the most? What have they been doing that is different from the others? Is that something you can share with the rest of the front-line leaders that report to you?

Actions to Take

■ Review with each of your supervisors what obstacles are causing their staff to lose time. Identify obstacles you can reduce or eliminate and do it or help your supervisors do it.
■ Review all the steps in your area. Find out from your supervisors what it would take to eliminate that step. See what you can do about it.

Chapter 9

Improvements in My Area

That Tuesday, Arthur, Peter, Farah, and I trooped into the conference room to meet with Julie. At least that's who we were expecting.

"What is this about, anyway?" asked Art as we assembled.

"I think Julie said it was Job Methodology or some'n like that," Peter answered. "Don't know nothin' more'n that. Some'n about methods. As if we don't know how to do this stuff in our sleep."

Then Sally and Yvonne came in. That was unexpected. Production doesn't usually mix with Sales much and although we work with Purchasing, there's not much interaction. It's like we're each in our own little world.

We said hi and chatted a bit until Julie strode in two minutes before the hour. There were a few words of banter. Then, somehow, right at 11, Julie shifted to business.

She started by saying that the skills she was going to introduce would be helpful everywhere in the company, and given that we would all have a lot to do in order to get the costs down in the next two months, she wanted us all to have the same perspective. Then she introduced something she said was called Job Methods. "The way they describe it is a bit archaic, and 75 years ago they didn't worry about gender-neutral language, but it's still worth hearing. The authors describe Job Methods as 'A plan to help the supervisor produce greater quantities of quality products in less time by making the best use of the manpower, machines and materials that are now available.'

"There are a few things I want to point out. First, this is for you in your areas. As you'll see, you have to connect with those around you, but primarily this is a method that's designed for you and your team to make improvements in your own areas.

"Second, you don't get anything more. You need to make improvements with the equipment and people you already have. Now that's not strictly true. You can scrounge. You can beg or borrow. You can jerry-rig stuff. And if the case is really compelling then we'll look at a bigger investment. My attitude is that you can spend up to $150 total for any project without asking my permission. And it doesn't need to succeed. But you do need to persuade at least two of your peers that the idea makes sense: the one you get material from, and the one you deliver it to. Treat it like your own money. Just keep the receipts and give them to me and you'll get reimbursed.

"Any questions about that?" There was silence.

Julie launched into the program. That first day she introduced us to the process of breaking a job down into all its little steps. As she described it, it seemed pretty simple. She walked us through a little demonstration of making toast in the lunch room that made it pretty easy to follow. We were astounded that making toast had four pages of details! (Figure 9.1 shows the first of the four pages.)

Then she sent us out to our own areas to observe an operation for ten minutes. We thought it would be pretty straightforward.

JOB DETAIL BREAKDOWN SHEET

PRODUCT: Toast	OBSERVATION MADE BY: Julie		DATE: April 1, 2019
OPERATIONS OBSERVED: Make Buttered Toast	DEPARTMENT: Kitchen		

Detail #	CURRENT/PROPOSED METHOD DETAILS	DISTANCE ft/m	REMARKS Time / Tolerance / Rejects / Safety	WHY/WHAT	WHERE	WHEN	WHO	HOW	IDEAS	ELIMINATE	COMBINE	REARRANGE	SIMPLIFY
1	Walk to fridge	10											
2	Remove bread, butter, jam		Struggled to carry all three	✓				✓	Butter stored on counter				
3	Walk to counter	10											
4	Place items on counter												
5	Open cupboard door												
6	Lift toaster to counter		Significant bend – low	✓					Best place for toaster?				
7	Close cupboard door												
8	Open bread bag		Twist tie took 10 turns – 2 the wrong way					✓	Replace twist tie with snap closer				
9	Remove 2 slices of bread and place on counter			✓	✓				Direct to toaster				
10	Close bread bag		4 turns of twist tie		✓				After toast down?				
11	Walk to cupboard	6		✓					After toast down?				
12	Open cupboard door			✓		✓			Cupboard door needed? After toast down?				
13	Lift down plate					✓			After toast down?				

Figure 9.1 The first page of the job detail breakdown Julie showed for making toast.

When we came back into the meeting room, we were all feeling pretty good about how it had gone. That was until Julie started leading us through what we had gathered. I realized I'd missed huge chunks of activity because I'd just assumed anyone would know it. Activities like moving a piece from one area of a workstation to another or putting the part down while preparing the mating piece, and then picking it up. Or listing a task as "set up the jig," because we were assuming that anyone would know to re-install the nuts, tighten them, and write down the observed settings on the machine. We just weren't picking up all the details.

By the time we had finished reviewing just two of the observations we were all laughing about how much we had missed. Julie pointed out that if we, who knew the work very well, couldn't list all the details accurately, how could we expect someone new to the work to do it correctly without a lot of guidance.

We also discovered that we did some silly things. Gil, for example. He runs the shipping area. He observed that when his folks boxed the product, they would write the order number on the outside of the box because the packing slip would go inside the box and be invisible. Then later, someone would print the shipping label, and they would match the shipping label to the number written on the box. All of a sudden, the reason for many of the shipping errors became clear. There was nothing in the process to tie the label to the box. Then, when the label was printed later it was easy for it to be placed on the wrong box. Of course, it resulted in the shipments going to the wrong customer.

"I'm going to fix that," Gil stated.

"And when you fix that," Julie asked, "how much do you think we'll save?"

Gil looked at her, clearly at a loss how to respond.

"I don't get it. I have no idea."

"Let's digress a bit, because this is something I want you all to be able to do," she started. "How often do we ship something to the wrong place?"

"Probably one or two times a week," Gil replied.

"Let's be conservative, and say it is once a week. Now, how much does it cost us to deal with a shipping error?"

"How would I know?" Gil responded.

"Gil, think it through. What happens?" Julie pressed him.

"Well, we get a call from a customer saying they received the wrong thing, or we get a call from a customer who didn't get anything, and we have to figure out what happened."

"And roughly how long does that take?"

"It depends," said Gil. There were snickers in the room.

"Of course it depends," countered Julie. "But I bet it doesn't take a day."

"No, of course not," Gil said defensively. "I guess most of the time we can sort it out in under an hour – maybe even 30 minutes."

"And are there some times you get lucky and figure it out in 5 minutes?" Gil nodded. Julie went on. "So, let's underestimate, and say 30 minutes. We know that our average hourly cost for people is about $28/hour, with all the extras loaded in. So that 30 minutes cost us $14.

"Now, how many of those shipping errors do you think are a result of what you noticed – that the shipping label doesn't match the packing slip inside the box?"

Gil thought for a moment. "I guess it's about two-thirds. I don't have data, and I know you like data, but when I think about it, that event happens more than half the time."

"And what other costs do we have?" Julie went on.

"Well, we have to ship the package back here, and ship the right stuff out to the person. Oh…" Gil's eyes lit up. "I can see where you're going with this. So if our average shipping cost is about $13, the extra shipping is $26."

Gil continued. "Then, we have to trace the other half of the mistake because there is almost always another parcel that has the label and picking slip mixed up. So we have to double everything. And then, of course, we have to pick the order again – actually both of them – and we know it costs us about $5 to pick and pack each parcel. So there is another $10.

"I guess then, we have $14 plus $13 for sorting it out and return shipping plus $13 for the replacement parcel, plus $5 for picking, and all of that times 2." He did some figuring on a scrap of paper. "That works out to… $90. And we have that maybe once a week or a bit more often …" He was silent as he did a quick calculation. "Wow. That's over $4,000 a year."

"Well done, Gil. Of course that is a minimum." Julie beamed. "Excellent job. Did the rest of you see how Gil did that?" There were nods around the room. "So can someone please explain what he did? Sally, can you try?"

Sally started with hesitation in her voice. "Well, it seems to me that he just listed all the extra steps that would need to be done to fix the problem, added up the cost of each one and then multiplied by how often we think it happens."

"Very well put, Sally," said Julie. She was smiling, and Sally smiled, too, and looked away. Sally was always uncomfortable being recognized or singled out.

Julie went on. "You can use this approach any time you make an improvement to figure out the impact, and it's good practice to do so.

In fact, in a couple of weeks I'm going to show you a form that will make it easy to do. But we're not there yet.

"The other thing I want you to take away from today, is this. How much will Gil's observation save us each year?"

Arthur piped up. He'd been quiet all morning. "Over four grand."

"Yes," confirmed Julie. "And we weren't even looking for anything. But this is pretty typical. My experience is that every time we go through the Job Methods process, we reduce annual costs by anywhere from $2,000 to $5,000, and sometimes it can be a lot more. I know one instance where the savings were $4,000 a month! That's a big deal.

"If each of you goes through this process once a quarter, with six of you, we can probably generate savings of $50,000–$70,000 per year. And it all goes right to the bottom line. And if you do it more often…?

"Well, that's enough for today. Here's your homework. I want you to do another observation between now and Friday. Come back then with the form filled out. My suggestion is that you do it in pairs. Having someone who doesn't know the process watch with you is usually helpful until you get some experience under your belts. It prevents you from missing details. Also, I need two volunteers who will go through their operation in detail in the next session."

After a bit of hesitation, Arthur and I volunteered.

"Any questions?" Julie finished up.

There was silence.

"Then I hope the rest of your day is great. Thanks to each of you." And then she was gone.

The six of us stood in the room looking at each other.

Yvonne broke the silence. "Wow! I've never had a class like that. But I still don't see how it applies to sales. I'm just making calls and sometimes, if they're local, making visits, but that's not very often. I've done a few over-night trips recently, but that's pretty new."

No-one offered any ideas.

There was some chit chat as some of us found partners for the observations we would do later in the week. Then the morning was done. I tidied up some details for the afternoon and went for lunch.

That Friday we were back in the room with Julie. Arthur and I were pretty pleased with ourselves. We'd each done our observations and we'd each found actions that just didn't make sense or that clearly presented opportunities for improvement.

Sally had paired with me. She told me it was the first time she'd ever really stopped to watch what we did on the floor. She asked some good questions, too, picking up on a couple of steps that I'd missed. I guess Julie was right about the value of new eyes.

Julie breezed into the room. She flashed a smile at each of us, greeted us, and got started. We each described what we'd observed. I had observed the CNC router in operation. Peter had looked at the kitting he did at the start of assembly. Gil had looked at the packing process when they had orders for single boats. Farah described her observation, how she and Alex took down the details when a customer wanted a new style of boat.

Then Sally spoke up. "I wasn't really sure what to do. I don't make anything. I just send orders to other people. And I do some calculations to figure out how much to order. But I don't actually make anything. So I haven't got anything to show you."

Yvonne was nodding. "Yeah. Me too. I'm doing sales. I make calls. I take orders. Sometimes if someone orders something online and it isn't clear, I'll call to clarify the order. And sometimes I'm prospecting, reaching out to potential new customers. Like last week when I got a lead on a guy with the pilots' association." We all smiled. Yvonne seemed so well suited to her job in sales. She could talk to anyone about anything.

"What's a pilot want with a boat? Boats got no wings." growled Arthur.

Yvonne laughed. "Not airplane pilots. Ships' pilots. These are the guys who direct the captain where to steer the boat as they come into harbour. Super highly paid. Imagine the cost if they make a mistake. Anyway, they thought it would be fun to have a pilot boat model they could give to members of the association when they get to 20 years or retire."

"Neat," Julie interjected. "So Sally, let's come back to your challenge. You can't see how this applies to you. Tell me. Are there some tasks that you do repeatedly?"

"Sure," said Sally. "Every day I probably send out half a dozen purchase orders [POs], and every day I probably order two or three items online."

"Well," Julie observed, "then you have repeating processes that you can observe and document. I should have realized you'd need more help than just our one example from last week. Paper and information processes are harder to see than physical processes." She turned to Yvonne. "I bet you had the same challenge as Sally." She paused, and Yvonne nodded. "So let's do one of these together as a group. You're all going to need to be able to do this."

Julie had us all go to Sally's desk. Weird. I wasn't used to classes where the instructor kept taking us to where the work was done. But she made some comment about how the workplace is the only place you can actually see what's happening. Then Julie gave us each one of the forms, and asked Sally to go through creating a couple of POs. As we watched and wrote down all the details that we were seeing, we began to see how moving information was just the same as moving material. Sally wrote down the PO number six times as she worked her way through the process. By the end it seemed silly, but there was a reason for each time. It was just inefficient. And we could all see a couple of ways she could eliminate the duplication. We saw it in her filing, too, where she had three copies of each PO in separate places, even though the original PO was still saved on the computer. She told us that it was just the way she'd been taught.

Julie brightened up. "This is so typical. People do things the way they're taught. That's a good thing, too. When any of us is learning, we're so overwhelmed that it's rare we can look at the process critically, so we just accept it as the way it is and move on. Then if we have the opportunity to look at it with fresh eyes, we see it doesn't make sense. The observations you do to fill in this form give you those fresh eyes."

By the time we were finished Sally had filled out the form and found several opportunities for improvement that she could do without affecting anyone else. But just as interesting, Yvonne mentioned that she was going to look at some of her procedures. She had some things in mind where she thought she could make a difference.

We headed back to the meeting room.

"I'm going to make a bit of a change," Julie started. "On Tuesday Arthur and Trevor agreed to present job breakdowns from their areas, but we have just helped Sally complete her form, so I'd like to carry on, if it's OK with you two." She nodded to the two of us. We each said that was fine, and she carried on. Then Julie led us through the complete analysis of Sally's process. It involved asking which parts of the process were causing difficulty, either because of errors or because it took a lot of effort, or because it was hard to learn. Then, for each of those parts of the process, we had to ask six questions:

1. Why do we do this detail? What is achieved?
2. What is the purpose of this detail?
3. Where is the best place to do this detail? Where else could it be done?
4. When is the best time to do this detail? When else could it be done?
5. Who is the best person to do this detail? Who else could do it? and
6. How is this detail done? How else could it be done? Which is the best way?

Then Julie pointed out that each of the questions pointed to particular kinds of improvement (Table 9.1).

Table 9.1   Job Methods (JM) Improvement Strategies

Question	Strategy	Question to Ask Yourself
Why? What?	Eliminate	Can we eliminate this detail?
Where? When? Who?	Combine/ Rearrange	Can we combine or rearrange details so it goes easier, faster or reduces errors?
How?	Simplify	Can we simplify how we do that detail?

She also gave us some ideas about the kinds of improvement we could think about. She put this table up on the whiteboard (Table 9.2).

Table 9.2   Examples of Job Methods (JM) Improvement Strategies

Strategy	Physical Examples	Information Examples
Eliminate	• Stop excess sanding • Automate counts	• Stop recording unused information • Reduce precision of measurements
Combine/Rearrange	• Consolidate tools • Use both hands • Place tools, parts near work	• Single instance of formulas • Collect all information at one point • Single filing location for data
Simplify	• Jigs or fixtures • Mistake proofing • Gravity feeds • Indexing	• Forms • Auto-correct or auto-validate • Drop-down menus • Category descriptions

Then she pointed out that we couldn't make these changes on our own. We had to get an OK from anyone doing the work, and we had to make sure that folks who received the work of our department would be OK with it, too.

We were all pretty amazed by the time we were finished. Sally had found four things she could change that would knock about 5 minutes off the time to do each PO. Over the course of the day, that would give her close to half an hour.

"What will you do with that half hour?" Julie asked.

"I'm not sure," Sally answered.

"What is the one thing you could do right now that would add the most value to the company?" Julie asked.

Sally thought for a minute. "Well, it seems to me that we've been having some late deliveries from some of our suppliers, and I hear that's causing some grief for production. Maybe I could use the time to start tracking on-time deliveries and giving some performance feedback to our suppliers."

"That's a really interesting idea, Sally." Julie went on. "What I'd like you to do is come up with half a dozen other ideas and then come back to me with your recommendation for which is the best. Can you do that for Monday afternoon?"

"Hey, Sally," Art offered, "what if you spent that time calling the suppliers who are supposed to deliver in a couple of days so they would get their act together and do it?"

"You can add that as one of the other ideas you consider," interjected Julie. "You OK with that, Sally?"

Sally agreed, and then Julie went on.

By the end of the session we'd been through one full round of the improvement process. We even got one of the changes Sally had in mind figured out enough that she wanted to talk to the people affected (mostly Neil) and get it ready to go for next week.

We didn't get to either Arthur's or my examples.

"Next week?" Julie asked brightly. We rolled our eyes in mock surprise. Of course it would be next week.

Later that day, I was surprised when Art came wandering into my part of the shop. "I canna' believe what Julie did," he started. I looked at him, questioning. "After the meetin', she came over to me and gave me a tongue lashing."

"What about?" I inquired.

"Well, she got all in a tizzy about my suggestion to Sally about callin' the suppliers."

"Really?" This didn't sound like Julie, but I've known Art for five years and he doesn't tell tales.

"Yeah. She said I wasn't bein' respectful."

"How so?"

"Oh, some garbage about how my comment that maybe the suppliers would get their act together and do what they were supposed to was disrespectful."

I wasn't sure how to respond. I could actually see Julie's point, though I didn't pick up on it at the time. Then I thought, let me get the facts. "Do you remember exactly what she said?"

Art paused for a bit, like he was dredging his memory. "Ummm. She said that my comment 'could be taken to mean that they're incompetent or that they're bein' malicious.'" He supplied the air quotes. "She also said that she didn't think it was what I meant, but she wanted us to speak about our suppliers with the same respect as if they were in the room."

"Doesn't sound so off base to me," I offered.

"Whose side are you on?" Art spat out his words.

"I don't think it's sides, Art. But I see her point. My Mum always told me that how we speak about someone when they're not in the room affects how we deal with them. Since we need those suppliers, we should probably speak about them nicely."

"But this is a bloody shop, Trevor. Hard words get spoken here. It's just how it is. Everyone knows we don't mean nothin' by it."

"I suppose. Still, I'm going to watch my language around Julie. She's been right about a lot of stuff, so I'm willing to give her the benefit of the doubt on this one, too."

Art mumbled an annoyed reply and headed back to the packaging area. I wondered how that was going to turn out. I knew Art from high school, and knew that he had come from a pretty rough family situation; he left home and stopped going to school when he turned 16. He found a job and supported himself from then on. Four years under Rocky hadn't softened any of his rough edges, but he was good to his crew and they knew it, even if his language was rough. I hoped he could adapt to Julie's expectations.

For the next few days I found myself looking at the work my team was doing and mentally breaking it down into every little step. Even at home, making toast or having my shower, or doing laundry, I found myself doing it. It got a bit annoying and rather amusing. I kept seeing extra motions in the work – things that weren't adding value, or that I didn't understand how they contributed to advancing the work. It made me start wondering how much of that stuff could be eliminated.

Since I was supposed to consult with the people who did the work, I pulled my team together for 15 minutes one morning, showed them what I was doing, and floated some questions I had. They got really excited when I went through the process with them, and then asked why we counted the pieces. It turns out that we counted the pieces because we wanted to match orders, and the operators couldn't keep track of the production count reliably as they were doing the work. But one of the team remembered seeing a person at his community centre using a count clicker to count the people attending events. "Why couldn't we use something like that, so we just click as we finish each part, or connect it to the machine?" I'd looked into it, and there were some inexpensive options available that could be mechanically linked to the machine cycle, so I was excited to add that to the ideas I'd present at the next session.

The next week both Art and I presented our operations and got through them. Art seemed to have got over his annoyance with Julie. For both of us we were able to streamline the operations way more than we'd imagined when we started. And it really helped to have the rest of the folks in the room there and helping. They really challenged our assumptions about how things had to be.

The idea of the counters was well received. Julie showed us how to complete a proposed change form, showing what we'd change, what the result would be, what the costs would be and what we'd save (Figure 9.2). It was pretty compelling, and Julie said to go ahead.

By the time we'd finished the five sessions, we were all feeling pretty comfortable with the Job Methods approach.

As we got to the end of the last day, Julie paused.

"This is a great tool," she started. "But it's like any tool. It has its place. It won't help us if we use it willy-nilly. You don't have time and the company doesn't have time to fix stuff that doesn't matter. While you were doing this learning, I wanted you to do a simple task so you could get used to the process. Now, we need to go back to what drove this effort. Anyone remember?"

"Sure," Arthur started. "You want us to cut costs by 15% so we can take that big order."

"That's part of it," Julie answered, "but it's more than taking that one order. If we can lower our costs, then we have more secure jobs, and more kids have smiles with our boats, and more people have the beauty of our boats in their lives.

"Now you have a tool that can help us get that 15%, so what I need you to do is look at your operations, pick the tasks that take the most effort, and apply the method to see what we can do.

"I'd like you to work in pairs. I'd like to hear from each of you in two days which operation you're going to work on, and who you will work with. Anyone see any obstacles to that?"

IMPROVEMENT PROPOSAL SHEET

Submitted to:	Julie	Date:		May 15, 2019
Prepared by:	Trevor	Company/Department:		Raw Stock
Product/Part:	Most			
Operation:	Counting at Chop Saw, CNC			

This is my proposal for improving how this work is performed.

Changes in Outcomes

Currently we count pieces after each production run. By putting in automatic counters we will pretty much eliminate over production and under production (people guess when to stop now), and it will typically reduce the cycle time for each work order by 2–3 minutes. With 3–15 work orders (WO) per day, it will free up 10–30 minutes (probably average 15 minutes) a day. On the chop saw, we can probably get one more work order done each day. On the CNC we will get about 4% more production.

	Before	After	Comment
Production per worker per day	CNC – 320	CNC– 335	Production min per day
Reject Rate	No change		May reduce damage
Cyle / Lead Time min	CNC – 57	CNC – 54	Cycle time for 1 WO
Other			

Specific Changes That Will Be Made to Achieve the Improved Outcomes

We will buy two mechanical resettable counters and fit them to the CNC and chop saw so that as each piece is ejected/removed from the machine, the counter goes up by one. The operator can see exactly how many pieces have been made on that run at any time.

The counters will require custom adapted brackets and will require Jamie to make or adapt some fingers that are located at the exit of the machine so they will increase the counter by one with each piece. Jamie estimates 2 hrs to make and install

Operators will reset the counter at the start of each work order. They can check the count and monitor production at any time until the work order is complete. The work order already allows for later errors, so no extra pieces need to be run. Remainders from raw stock will be returned to the stock shelves as they are now.

Each counter will cost under $50, the brackets will cost under $20 in material, and it will take Jamie one hour to install each one. Total $200
Minimum cost reduction is 15 minutes/day x $28/staff hr x 2 machines = $15/day
Cost payback — three weeks.

Individuals Who Have Contributed to This Proposal:
Teyjas, Jas, Jamie, Sylvie

Figure 9.2 The Job Methods (JM) proposal form prepared by Trevor for installing counters on the machines.

No-one said anything, and there were head nods all around.

"Great. I'm looking forward to hearing about what you find."

And with that, she was on her way.

***

Three weeks later we had each completed our first projects.

I'd looked at the machine set-up for our moulder. We made several different-sized dowels for the different boats, and the change-over took over two hours to complete. By using the Job Methods process, we realized that there were many parts of the task we could do in advance, before the machine actually stopped. I later learned this process was called single-minute exchange of die, or SMED. It turns out there is a whole science to the process. It really helped when Julie suggested we think about the operation in four parts: get ready, changeover, work and put-away. The upshot was that we took over an hour out of each set-up. It took us a few tries to get there, but everyone was on board, and it stayed pretty stable. It gave us 2 hours a day more production time, which meant that our costs for those dowels went down by almost 25%, and we could produce more. Julie insisted that we document the change by creating a Job Instruction Breakdown Sheet for each of the four parts of the operation.

The others all found similar improvements. Julie pushed us to give it another go with another process, and we got similar results. In the end, we actually dropped our costs by about 18%. It meant that our overtime went down and everyone pretty much left on time at the end of the day, which was a nice change.

Meanwhile Yvonne had been applying the same processes to her sales work, and she was now making more calls, which meant that our orders were going up, and we actually had to hire another person.

Reflecting on the Chapter

For Supervisors (overseeing front-line workers)

- What are the last three improvements made in your area? Who was involved? What is better because of those improvements?
- What is your authority to make changes in work processes when they only affect your area? What approvals are needed? What information or forms do the people doing approving need completed so they will agree?
- How does your current organization respond to mistakes? Are they celebrated? Are they tolerated? Do people get fired? Do people learn from them?
- Are there people in your organization who do "stealth improvements" (improvements that involve changes without official authorization or permission)? If so, how do they get away with it? What kinds of improvements do they do?
- Look at the problem Trevor was dealing with regarding counting parts. How many other ways can you see to address his problem and eliminate the counting process?

Actions to Take

- Download copies of the blank form from Figure 9.1 to record all the details of a task in your area. Go to www.becomingthesupervisor.com/ downloads.
- Identify the details that are hard to do or that have lots of rework associated with them or that take a long time. Apply the six questions in Table 9.1 to each of those details to see what improvements you can make. Use Table 9.2 to give you some ideas of how you can improve the details.
- Watch an important operation in your area for 45 minutes or two full cycles. Identify steps or motions that could be made easier for the operator(s). Speak to the people doing the work and find out what drives them to do the work the way they do it. What are the obstacles to doing it an easier way?

CAUTION: Use the form in Figure 9.1 only to work on improvements, not for instruction. There is so much detail that it will confuse the learner if you use the form for instruction. Also, this form doesn't include the information about key points – how to do the detail correctly.

For Managers *(you have supervisors or managers reporting to you)*

Consider all the questions for supervisors for yourself. Then consider the following.

■ What roadblocks do your supervisors face if they want to make local improvements (improvements that don't cost money)?
■ How did your predecessor deal with mistakes and/or improvements and/or initiatives?
■ If you could make local improvements to one of your production processes, what would it be?

Actions to Take

■ Watch an operation together with each of your supervisors, and together, document every detail of the operation. Pick three to five problematic details (takes a long time, high rework, hard to learn, dangerous) and use the six questions to find opportunities to make improvements. Have each supervisor discuss the changes with their respective teams and reach agreement. Then champion any proposed changes through the approval process. Ensure that the benefit of the changes are documented on an Improvement Proposal Form (Figure 9.2), and ensure that new instructions are recorded on Job Instruction Breakdown Sheets (Figure 7.4) and presented to your boss by the supervisors and their teams.

Chapter 10

The Problem Child

It was late in the day in the midst of the improvement work that I'd been doing when I got the first hint that something was amiss. Sunil approached me as I was watching an operation. My crew were pretty used to me doing that now, and mostly ignored me. But Sunil came up to me, glanced around, and said, "Trevor? You gotta minute?"

"Sure," I responded. Sunil was usually so quiet and said so little that if he wanted to talk, I needed to listen. Besides, I had watched this operation many times, and I couldn't see anything different. I closed my notebook and turned to Sunil. "What's up?"

"You go see Zhou. You see."

"What will I see, Sunil." I didn't want to be going anywhere on a witch hunt. I'd seen staff trying to play their supervisor before, and I knew there had been friction between the two of them.

"Very bad work. Very bad. Many mistakes. Lots of garbage. Makes me slow."

"What mistakes, Sunil."

"Very bad. Many mistakes."

"Look, Sunil, you need to tell me what you're seeing. I don't understand what's happening."

"You look, Trevor. You see yourself."

This was going 'round and 'round'. I wasn't getting anything from him. After a few more exchanges with no better results I was getting frustrated. "Look Sunil, I'm sure you're seeing something, but until you can be more specific, I'm not going on a witch hunt. You come and tell me when you can show me the problem or when you can describe it better."

With that, I turned and walked off to my office.

"You see," Sunil spoke loudly. "Very bad. Very very bad."

Yeah, sure, I thought to myself. I'm not going to fall into that trap. A supervisor being played by their workers is not pretty. I was pretty sure he was trying to play me. I didn't give it much thought.

A couple of days later, Peter from assembly came over to find me. "Come and see this, Trev," he invited. I walked over to the assembly area with him. He picked up one of the freighters we make in one hand, and with the other he wiggled the funnel.

The funnel is just a piece of dowel that is rounded at the end. It should fit quite snugly into the cabin, so it takes some pressure to get it in. That helps the glue hold, and it helps the finish really seal the joint. I guess it wouldn't be surprising if you have kids, but I was always surprised to see kids carrying their boats by the funnel. The funnels take a lot of abuse, so they have to fit well.

"Trev, we started seeing these about two days ago. At first it wasn't too bad, but it's been getting worse and worse as we've worked our way through this batch. Now they're so consistently bad that we can't use them. I need you to make a couple of hundred, and if I'm going to get these finished on time, I need the funnels by 9 tomorrow morning."

"Sure, Peter. I'll get right on it. Any idea whether it's the cabin or the funnel that's out of spec?"

"I'm not sure. But my guess is it's the hole. Look! Just looking at it you can see that it is a bit oval. But I don't have my callipers here to measure with. We just expect the parts to be correct when we get them."

"Fair enough," I answered. "Let me take a dozen or so of each with me."

I took the parts with me. It took about five minutes with my callipers to see that the problem was the hole. It was too big by less than 1/100th of an inch in one direction which might have been tolerable, except that in the other direction the hole was 6/100ths of an inch too big (almost 1/16"). No wonder we could see it. But how would we be making a hole that far from true? And why wouldn't the operator have caught it?

I was clearly going to have to track down the operator and have a word with whoever it was.

It didn't take long to figure out that the person who made these cabins was Zhou. I went looking for her. This was not the first time we'd had quality problems from her. I could feel my blood beginning to boil.

Zhou was working at the drill press again. "Zhou!" I barked. Her head came up as she turned to me. If I'd been paying attention, I'd have seen the fear in her face. "What were you thinking, passing along these pieces to assembly," I started, exasperated. "You know the holes have to be tight." I held up one of the pieces I had in my hand. "Look. They're all the same. Totally unacceptable. You know better, Zhou." I was getting worked up, talking louder and louder. In the corner of my eye I saw Marcus on the forklift watching. "You can do better than this," I went on. "And this is just the most recent problem with your work. I can't think how many times I've had to talk to you about quality, and this is just one more example. I won't have it any more." I stopped for breath.

Zhou was looking very timid. "But Mr. Trevor," she was almost pleading. "Drill press no good. I told you very hard to make good. I told you make it on CNC."

"I don't need any of your excuses, Zhou. You know how to make it right and you're just not paying attention. I'm not interested in making it easier for you. I'm interested in you making the parts right. You need to be way more careful. You do any more stupid things like making bad parts and I'm going to write you up."

Zhou looked at me wide-eyed. "But Mr. Trevor. Machine no good. Better to do it on CNC."

"I don't care where you think it should be done. I made those parts on that machine for years. The machine is fine. You need to be more careful. Make them again, and make it quick. Peter needs 200 by tomorrow at 9:00." I glared at her, turned, and walked away.

Even as I walked away I had this sinking feeling that the exchange had not gone well. Yeah. I'd vented my frustration. Zhou knew what she needed to do. But something under my skin was crawling.

Within the hour Julie came to find me. "Come with me, Trevor," was all she said. She was stone-faced. I didn't know where we were going, but I was pretty sure I wasn't going to like this. She didn't wear that hard expression often – most of the time she was really easy-going.

We got to the conference room, went in, and she shut the door.

"Trevor, what happened with you and Zhou?"

"Zhou made 200 bad cabins and just passed them along to Assembly. They won't work and I told her that bad parts aren't acceptable, and she needs to be more careful, and she needs to re-make the 200 parts for tomorrow by nine o'clock."

"Tell me about how you spoke to her," she directed.

"I was mad. I guess I raised my voice a bit. This is probably the fifth or sixth time she's made bad parts in the last month. She's just not paying attention, and we can't have that, so yeah, I was pretty annoyed."

"You were annoyed. So you looked after your own feelings and didn't think about the feelings of your team member." She stopped.

"What do you mean? What do her feelings have to do with it? She made a mistake and she needs to know about it and fix it."

"Let me give you a direct instruction, Trevor. You are never to blow up at your people. Ever. Ever. Do you understand?" She was speaking slowly and very distinctly.

"OK" I responded, warily. Maybe there was even a bit of a question in my voice.

"I don't think you got this." Julie's voice was flat – hard – like cold steel. Like nothing would ever take it off the same dead tone. "Tell me what I just directed you."

"You told me not to blow up at my people."

"That's right. Now here is my second direct instruction. You will always correct people in private." She paused. "Again, tell me what I've just directed you."

"I'm not to correct anyone in front of others."

"Good try. You will do correction in private. Try again."

"I'm only to correct people in private."

"That's it. Now that you have stated what I'm expecting, let me tell you what I've learned since you blew up at Zhou.

"If you are angry or annoyed or frustrated, those are your feelings. You're entitled to them. But you are not entitled to embarrass your people. Do you remember what your two primary jobs are?"

I'd heard this so many times now, that I knew the answer. "Achieve the mission of the organization, and look after my people."

"Right. So how is blowing up at your people looking after them?"

"OK. But what about Zhou's mistakes? I can't have her making bad parts."

"No-one said anything about tolerating bad work. Like I won't tolerate bad work from my supervisors, like blowing up at their people. I didn't blow up at you, but I bet you're clear that I think you did bad work?"

"Yeah," I said, weakly.

"And are you clear now what I'm expecting?"

"Yeah," I responded quietly. "Not to blow up at my people."

"And what else?"

"Ummm…" I was trying to remember. But I was so nervous I couldn't recall. "Something about correcting my people."

"OK. Let's go over that again. You are to correct people in private. Where?"

"In private."

"Right. So I have just demonstrated to you what I expect. Now I am going to tell you why this is important.

"I don't know how much you know about non-white cultures. My family has mostly been in this country for five generations, but my grandfather came from China from a small village. You know my last name?"

"Yes," I answered. "Cheng."

"What you don't know is that my grandmother's family name is Zhou. Same as Zhou's. In fact you all call her by her family name, because when she arrived here she didn't have an English-sounding name, and she found people had too much trouble with her given name. She came from the same village as my grandmother, so when I heard her accent all I could think of was my grandmother. So I can understand her very well. Can't speak it much anymore, but she can talk to me.

"She told me that the way you spoke to her in public she wanted to walk out of the company and never come back. She felt she had been humiliated in front of her colleagues. She had experienced what is loosely translated as losing face. In her eyes, she had had all respect for her stripped away by your actions. She stewed about it for an hour and was about to walk out of the plant when I ran into her. Fortunately, she trusts me enough to tell me about what happened. I was able to reassure her that there was still a place for her in this company, and that she would continue to be trusted by me."

"If I had not been there, your blow-up – your loss of self-control – would have cost the company a good worker. And you already know how hard it is to find good workers. We can't afford to lose people like her.

"I haven't even begun to talk about the damage your actions have caused among the others. What does Marcus think now? Is he going to be more or less comfortable about his position in the company, having seen how you treated Zhou?"

What could I say? "I suppose he'll be less comfortable."

"You bet. And if he is less comfortable, is he going to be more or less productive?"

"Less." By this point I was beginning to feel terrible. Yet in all this time, Julie had never once raised her voice, or expressed anything other than full respect for me.

"So you have to fix this problem. Neither you nor the company can afford to have people afraid for their position, or be less productive."

"But I don't know how to fix this problem," I countered. "I know I messed up, but how do I fix it?"

"Smartest thing you've said this conversation," smiled Julie. "So you'd like to learn how? Let me introduce you to a method that will help you. Let's start with a question. What is your objective in this situation?"

"I'm not sure I understand your question. I want Zhou to like me, and I want her to produce what I need."

"Hmmm. Is your objective really that you want Zhou to like you? Let me ask you a different question. Do you think that I'd have had this conversation with you if I wanted you to like me?"

"No."

"Certainly not. And although it is actually only a true friend that will have hard conversations with someone, my job is not to have you like me. My job is to make sure you are capable of doing what the company needs so it can achieve its mission, and I have to look after my people – all of you. I'm not that fussed about whether you like me or not. Because there are times I need to have hard conversations with you, and I can't avoid those because I'm worried about whether you'll like me.

"So let's come back to my first question. What is your objective for Zhou?"

"Hmmm." Was I copying Julie? "Well I do want Zhou to produce what I need, and I need her not to make so many mistakes."

"Given what you know, that's probably an OK set of objectives. Do you see that these line up with your two big responsibilities: look after the mission, and look after your people?"

"I hadn't, but I see it now that you point it out."

"It's a good test about whether you have good objectives. Now, what facts do you know about the situation?"

"Well, Zhou made 200 parts wrong. And it's about the sixth time this month."

"What else do you know?"

"What more is there to know?" I asked.

"Are these mistakes new for her, or has this been going on for a long time?"

"It's new."

"So what has changed?"

"I don't know." I shrugged.

"Don't you think you should know?" Julie pushed.

"I'm not sure it matters, does it?" I asked.

"Let me present a situation and you tell me if it matters. A worker makes great parts. Then over time he makes more and more mistakes. Then the worker gets glasses for the first time and the mistakes go away. Did it matter that the mistakes were new?"

"Yeah. If someone had figured out that he couldn't see well, the situation could have been fixed sooner."

"Exactly." Julie smiled. "So if the mistakes are new for Zhou, doesn't that at least raise a suspicion that something else might have changed, other than assuming that Zhou didn't care anymore?"

"I guess."

"It should. And asking whether the situation is new is an excellent question to trigger that curiosity. What else do you know?"

"I'm not sure."

"Do you know if there has been any change in the materials or the machine?"

"No."

"Do you know if others have been making more mistakes of a similar nature?"

"Well, now that you mention it, I know the last time Sylvie ran something on that machine she had to re-run several of the parts."

"So that is a fact that you need to include in your analysis. Now, here's what you just told me." She pushed a piece of paper toward me. Down one side she had written:

- Zhou made 200 parts wrong
- Sixth time this month
- Before this month she didn't make many mistakes
- Sylvie had to re-run several parts on the machine
- Don't know what has changed
- Don't know about material
- Don't know about machine

When she wrote it down it was pretty obvious what I needed to deal with.

"So I guess I need to find out about those things."

"Yes. But before you rush off, a couple more questions." I didn't know whether to be exasperated at Julie or amazed. She always has more questions. Sometimes I wish she'd just tell me stuff. But she always does it in such a nice way that it feels like it would be unreasonable to resist.

She continued. "If you just go ask Zhou about this, do you think she is going to give you a straight answer?"

"What do you mean? Why wouldn't she?"

"Do you think she trusts you or fears you right now?"

"Oh." I was crestfallen. Of course. How could I be so thick. "Yeah. She'll be afraid."

"And when you're afraid, are you at your best?"

"Not at all."

"So you have some other facts." She added to the list. Now it looked like this.

- Zhou made 200 parts wrong
- Sixth time this month
- Before this month she didn't make many mistakes
- Sylvie had to re-run several parts on the same machine
- Don't know what has changed
- Don't know about material
- Don't know about machine
- Trevor blew up at Zhou
- Zhou feels she lost face
- Zhou was going to walk out of the plant
- Zhou told Julie she was afraid of Trevor

"When you look at this list now, does it change your objectives at all?"

"I guess so. I need to get Zhou so she's OK about me."

"Yup. Because one of your two responsibilities is look after what…?"

"My people."

"Exactly. You have to look after your people."

"So in summary, you have an employee you blew up at after she made bad parts. The mistakes are new for her. Another employee also made bad parts on the same machine in the last month. You don't know if anything has changed. The employee feels she has lost face, and is now afraid of her supervisor.

"Does that pretty much describe it in about 50 words?"

"Yeah. That pretty much says it."

"And what are your objectives now?"

"I want Zhou to feel like she has restored respect, and I want to stop the mistakes at the drill press."

"Much better, Trevor. Here's what we've just done. We've identified the objective, and we've gathered the first round of facts on this situation. You've identified that you have more facts to gather, and you have identified an excellent objective for Zhou – that she feels like her respect has been restored.

"So, what are your options for action now?"

"I don't get the question. I need to figure out what's going on at the drill press."

"Sure. But is there more than one way to do that?"

"I guess so. Does it really…" I was going to say "matter" and then I stopped. I could see where Julie would take this. Of course it mattered. Because Zhou was still afraid. "Oh, Yes. It does matter. Because just finding out about the drill press doesn't deal with Zhou, does it?" I asked tentatively.

"Well done, Trevor. You've got it. You have to keep both objectives in mind, and some actions will be more helpful than others. You need to sort that out. I need to make a quick call right now to delay a meeting. I'll need two minutes – maybe three. While I'm gone, I want you to come up with eight possible actions you could take."

"OK," I replied. Then she was gone.

I got five options pretty quickly, and then I got stumped.

1. Talk to Zhou about drill press and raw material
2. Talk to Sylvie about drill press and raw material
3. Talk to others who might have used drill press
4. Ask Sally if there had been any changes in wood supply
5. Ask Peter if there had been any other problems with parts from the drill press

I looked at the page the rest of the time that Julie was gone. Nothing came. Then moments before she walked in the door I had an idea and wrote down:

6. Apologize to Zhou

I was still two short.

Julie came in and asked how it went.

"I got six" I started. "Actually I got five easily, and only got the sixth just before you came back."

"Good start. You know what's next, eh?" She smiled at me. "More questions!" She laughed. "Could you ignore the situation?"

"That's a terrible option," I protested.

"Didn't ask if it was a good option. Only asked if you could ignore it."

"Of course."

"It's not that I'm recommending it for this situation, but sometimes it's a good option – sometimes even the best." Julie exhaled. "Next question.

If you apologize to Zhou, does that fix the situation for her and Marcus, who watched the whole blow-up?"

"No. But I have no idea how I'd do that." I hesitated, then decided to ask. "What would you do?"

"One option that occurs to me is that you could do a public apology after you have done the private one. Does that give you something to work with?"

"I like that. It won't be easy but I think Zhou would feel that it honoured her."

"Another option is that you apologize to Zhou, then figure out what was really happening and do all that before the public apology."

"Oh wow. How do you come up with these ideas?"

"I've been doing this for several years now. I don't have to reinvent a lot of the ideas. So you have eight options now. You need to figure out which one or two would be best. Would you like some guidance, or are you OK to do that on your own?"

"I think I can figure out what to do on my own."

"OK. Do that, but before you take any action, I want you to come back to me and show me your plan. And I want to see it by tomorrow at 9. You don't have a lot of time to fix this."

I agreed and headed on my way. By then there was less than half an hour until the end of the shift. They were the longest 30 minutes I can remember. It felt like there was this great cloud on me. I was so aware of how I'd messed up, and of how I had humiliated Zhou and I kept wondering what my team were thinking as I went through my end-of-shift routine. No one said anything, but no one looked me in the eye either. It was super uncomfortable.

That night I phoned Beth, my sister. She always has such a good head on her shoulders about these things. I explained the whole story. She was sympathetic, but she was really hardnosed. "Buck up kid. This is just like when Dad used to make us apologize for annoying the neighbours when we fought. Do you remember?" Did I ever. We'd have to go over together to their door, knock on their door, and then, when they came to the door we'd have to apologize.

"Good evening Mrs. Thirkell. We're here to apologize for disturbing your evening with our fighting and screaming. We know it must have been really annoying after your day at work. If we're upset with each other again, we'll go inside to sort it out. Please accept our apologies." Of course, they always did, and four times out of five they'd offer us cookies, but we would dutifully decline – at least we did after the first time when Dad found out that we'd got cookies from her.

"No way, kiddos," he'd say. "You don't get to benefit from an apology. The apology is for you to acknowledge that you messed up, not for you to get rewarded."

Yeah, I'd had some experience apologizing. So my sister was great and insisted that I practice with her until I'd got the words down.

After my call with her, I wrote down my plan.

1. Apologize privately to Zhou for correcting her in public
2. Find out about the machine – what had other operators experienced
3. Verify the raw material situation
4. Draw some conclusions
5. Come up with a plan
6. Apologize to Zhou in front of the team and share the plan

That night I hardly slept. At some point in the night I remembered Sunil's comments from a couple of days ago. Suddenly I wondered if he was trying to warn me about the parts. Maybe he wasn't really trying to get Zhou in trouble. Maybe he was trying to save my skin. And I had just brushed him off – dismissed him. But I didn't know. I got up, turned on the light and re-wrote my plan.

1. Apologize privately to Zhou for correcting her in public
2. Apologize to Sunil for dismissing him, for not listening
3. Find out what Sunil wanted to tell me
4. Find out about the machine – what had other operators experienced
5. Verify the raw material situation
6. Draw some conclusions
7. Come up with a plan
8. Apologize to Zhou (and maybe Sunil) in front of the team and share the plan

I went in early that morning. I was waiting for Julie when she arrived. She greeted me brightly. "Good evening?" she asked.

"Not really. Didn't sleep well at all. But I guess it was OK because I had another insight about an exchange with Sunil." I went on to explain what happened. Then I showed her my revised plan.

"Wow. This is a really detailed plan. It's a good starting point. A caution for you, though. You can only count on doing the first three. By then you'll have learned some new things, and that will change your plan. But you're certainly going in the right direction. Have you ever apologized to someone that reports to you one-on-one before?"

I hadn't.

"Let me give you a few words of advice.

1. Be explicit about what you did wrong
2. Don't qualify it
3. Don't make excuses
4. Don't bury it in other stuff
5. Don't expect anything in return
6. Explain what you are going to do to set the relationship right – what you will do to make amends or what you will do differently. If you're not sure yet, tell them you aren't sure what you need to do. You can ask *them* if they want you to do something"

I recognized everything my parents had taught Beth and me in Julie's points.

"Here's what I want you to do. Have those first three conversations. And figure out what's going on with the machine. Then come back and see me. I'm glad to see that you did this work last night. You don't have a lot of time to fix this."

"One more thing. I'd suggest you not say anything about a public apology until you are very clear what you're going to do. I also suggest that you speak with both Zhou and Sunil to make sure they know what you're going to say before you say it to the others. You're not ready to do that yet."

The apologies were so hard for me to do. I felt so embarrassed. And looking back, I should have been feeling that way. I dreaded them as I walked to Zhou and then to Sunil. But once I'd actually said the apologies and explained that I intended to do a better job of listening by not interrupting people, and explained that I was going to figure out what was really going on, well, it felt like this weight was off me.

Then I went after the problem. I went back to the production records and saw that Zhou's error rate was no different than anyone else's. She just did more work on the drill press than anyone else. So I asked Zhou to show me what was happening with the drill. She showed me how the drill wobbled – clearly at least one of the bearings in the drill had failed. I guessed that the off-and-on nature of the wobble initially was the bearing starting to fail. And as the bearings got worse, the wobble got worse. I tagged the drill press out of service. When I talked to Sunil, he said that he'd seen the wobble starting, and that's what he was trying to tell me. But in my impatience, in my assumptions about his motivation, I'd dismissed his information.

By 10 that morning I had tracked down Julie. I explained what I'd learned. "I feel ashamed," I went on. "The problem had nothing to do with Zhou, and everything to do with the machine."

"Does this change your list of eight possible actions?"

"It sure does. I figured you'd ask, so I redid them."

I handed her my new list.

1. Do nothing
2. Get the drill press fixed
3. Apologize to Zhou and Sunil in front of the team
4. Teach the operators how to change bearings
5. Get our maintenance person to do a better job checking the machines
6. Get Peter to have his people check the parts when they arrive at Assembly
7. Figure out a way to track errors better so we catch them sooner
8. Get the operator to check the spindle at the start of every shift

I told her it took me a long time to come up with the last two.

"Do you have a plan?"

"I think so. I'll do No. 3 and No. 2, but I couldn't decide between whether to do No. 5 or No. 6 or No. 7."

"Let's go back to your objectives. Do your objectives still make sense, given what you've learned?"

I hesitated. I'd forgotten what my objectives were. I pulled out my notes and saw what I'd written: Zhou not to make so many mistakes, and Zhou and Sunil to know that they are respected. Then I realized that those really weren't my objectives any more. I needed to fix the drill press, and I needed to catch machines that were failing sooner in the cycle, and there was something else but I wasn't sure what.

"I know that I've got some objective with Zhou, but I'm not sure how to put it down."

"Ask yourself, 'What behaviour do I want from her?' What is it that you need her to do that she hasn't been doing."

"Well, I guess what I need her to do is let me know right away if she's having trouble with the machines. If I'd heard about this a month ago, maybe we'd have avoided this."

"Maybe," she replied. "Maybe not. You've learned something about listening since then. But you're right that you want to know. So you might need to frame an objective around that. But before you focus on Zhou, was she the only one who worked on that machine and didn't say anything?"

"Ohhhh. I see what you're getting at. I need that behaviour from everyone on any machine. And none of my actions do anything about that."

"Exactly." Julie was smiling. "So what is your plan now?"

"I guess I need to get the drill press fixed, and then I need to have a conversation with my team and apologize to Zhou and Sunil, and state my expectation to everyone that if they find a machine that isn't operating properly, they have to let me or whoever is the acting supervisor know."

"Pretty good. You may also want to speak to the drill press operators as a group first. Because they are the ones who didn't do what you need in the first place. In general, when you have someone who has done something you don't want, it's a good idea to speak to them directly before you make the more general request. Then it's more likely to land. Are you OK to carry out your plan now?"

"I think so, but maybe if you could be at the meeting with the whole team, you'd be able to give me some feedback. I haven't done this stuff much."

Julie agreed and we lined up a time 45 minutes later. I spoke to the drill press operators, and then a few minutes later, to the whole team. It felt like the whole atmosphere brightened a bit as I did my apology.

Afterwards, Julie pulled me over. "You did a good job with your apology, Trevor. No excuses. It's been a rough couple of days for you. I hope you feel like you've learned something."

"Sure have."

"What I led you through – the thinking process – is actually a structured approach. It comes from a program called Job Relations. I figured you just needed to get through it, rather than learn all the little bits and pieces. So I have a couple of things for you. The first is a Job Relations card (Figure 10.1). It has all the important steps and key points for how to deal with a situation where people aren't performing the way you need them to. It's also not a bad guide to general problem solving. The second is a form I've found really helpful. It gives you space for the whole thinking process on a single page, from setting your objective to getting the facts, weighing your options and deciding – planning your action, and planning for your follow-up (Figure 10.2).

Sussex Creek
B O A T W O R K S

JOB RELATIONS

Set Your Objective

STEP 1 – GET THE FACTS

1. Review the **RECORD** (good and bad)
2. Find out what **CUSTOMS & RULES** apply
3. Talk with the **INDIVIDUAL** concerned
4. Get **OPINIONS** and **FEELINGS**

Be sure you have the whole story!

STEP 2 – WEIGH AND DECIDE

1. Fit the facts **TOGETHER**
2. Consider their **BEARINGS** on each other
3. Check **POSSIBLE ACTION**
4. Check **PRACTICES** and **POLICIES**
5. Consider the **OBJECTIVE** and the **EFFECTS** on the individual, the group and on production

Be careful not to jump to conclusions.

STEP 3 – TAKE ACTION

1. Are you going to do it **YOURSELF**?
2. Do you need **HELP** handling it?
3. Should you **REFER** it to your Supervisor?
4. Watch the **TIMING**

Don't pass the buck.

STEP 4 – CHECK RESULTS

1. How **SOON** will you follow up?
2. How **OFTEN** will you need to check?
3. Watch for **CHANGES** in output, attitude and relationships.

Did your actions help production?

DID YOU ACHIEVE YOUR OBJECTIVE?

Sussex Creek
B O A T W O R K S

JOB RELATIONS

A Supervisor gets results through people.

FOUR FOUNDATIONS
FOR GOOD RELATIONS

1. **Let each worker know how he/she is getting along**
   - Figure out what you expect and tell them
   - Point out ways to improve
   - Start with curiosity (not blame)

2. **Give credit when due**
   - Look for extra or unusual performance
   - Tell the person while it's "hot"
   - Be specific

3. **Tell people in advance about changes that will affect them**
   - Tell them why if possible
   - Work with them to adjust to the change

4. **Make best use of each person's ability**
   - Look for abilities not now being used
   - Never stand in a person's way

PEOPLE MUST BE TREATED AS INDIVIDUALS

Figure 10.1   The TWI Job Relations card Julie created for Sussex Creek Boatworks.

"The only thing that needs any explaining is that once you have all the facts written down, draw a solid line between any of the facts that make sense together, and draw either a dotted line or use another colour to connect the facts that seem to contradict each other. So if you have a worker who hasn't made many mistakes in the past and is now making lots, you'd put a dashed line between them. Or if you have the facts that a person is often late, and the others are complaining, those two seem to fit together, so use a solid line to connect them. I've found that if I do this, it makes it easier for me to summarize at the bottom.

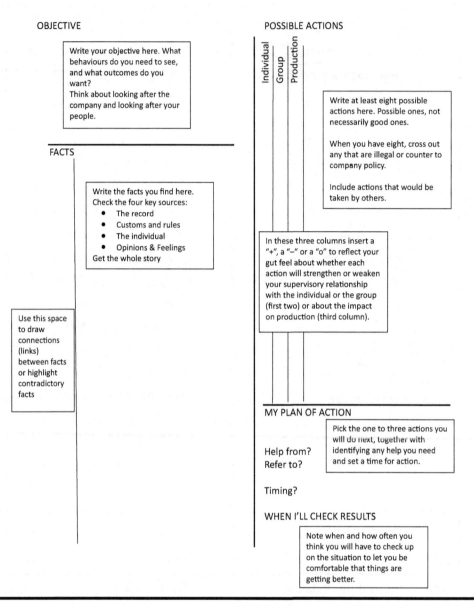

Figure 10.2   The Job Relations (JR) worksheet template Julie gave to Trevor.

"My task right now is to set my follow-up with you. Because you see I had two objectives in the last two days: I needed to see that your relationship with Zhou got fixed – and Sunil once I learned about that – because I need you to be an effective supervisor. And I needed you to learn how to handle a situation like this the next time it comes up – and it will – so we don't lose production.

"So now for the follow-up." Julie and I talked about how soon the drill press could be fixed and agreed on a date. Then we talked about what I'd do to follow up with Zhou and Sunil to make sure those relationships were repaired, and with the rest of the team to make sure they understood the importance of reporting machines that weren't working. Again, we agreed on some dates.

Just as I thought we were done, Julie said, "Two more things."

"First, I'd like to schedule some time with you next week. I want to go over this method with you more formally. It's such a critical tool in your supervisor toolbox that I want you to be really solid in it." We set a time.

"Second, the next time you run into a situation where someone isn't performing the way you need, I want you to complete this worksheet, and come to me with it and your plan, so we can go over it, and I want to see it before you do anything. Got it?"

I got it. She was very clear. We each went on our way.

That night I called my sister and told her how it went. It was a relief that it was over and I told her that.

"Yeah," she said, "for the moment."

"What do you mean, sis?"

"Come on, Trevor. You've always reacted pretty fast. You'll get yourself in hot water again, I'm sure. It's just who you are. But at least now you have a way to get out of it. That's pretty cool. And I think I'd like you to show me this card that Julie gave to you. I've got one of my staff that I have a problem with."

We planned to have dinner together that weekend, and hung up.

That night I slept like a log.

Three weeks later, Sylvie, who is charming but not super reliable on the attendance front, was late again. She'd had a pretty good month, with only one other late, but it was still an issue. It had been an issue since I first became a supervisor. So I filled in the worksheet (Figure 10.3). Then I set a time to meet Julie. She looked it over, nodding as she did.

"Pretty good," she commented. "I can see that you've checked all four core sources: the individual, records, customs and rules, and opinions and feelings. You've connected the facts that fit together, and the ones that don't seem to fit. And I can see you have a good range of options. What I can't see is how you reached the choices you made for your plan."

I talked through how I'd thought about each option.

"Would you like a faster and more consistent way to sort through the options?"

"Sure," I replied.

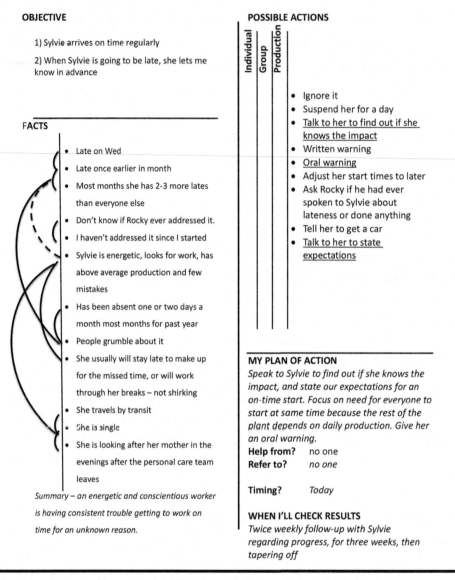

OBJECTIVE

1) Sylvie arrives on time regularly

2) When Sylvie is going to be late, she lets me know in advance

FACTS

- Late on Wed
- Late once earlier in month
- Most months she has 2-3 more lates than everyone else
- Don't know if Rocky ever addressed it.
- I haven't addressed it since I started
- Sylvie is energetic, looks for work, has above average production and few mistakes
- Has been absent one or two days a month most months for past year
- People grumble about it
- She usually will stay late to make up for the missed time, or will work through her breaks – not shirking
- She travels by transit
- She is single
- She is looking after her mother in the evenings after the personal care team leaves

Summary – an energetic and conscientious worker is having consistent trouble getting to work on time for an unknown reason.

POSSIBLE ACTIONS

Individual | Group | Production

- Ignore it
- Suspend her for a day
- Talk to her to find out if she knows the impact
- Written warning
- Oral warning
- Adjust her start times to later
- Ask Rocky if he had ever spoken to Sylvie about lateness or done anything
- Tell her to get a car
- Talk to her to state expectations

MY PLAN OF ACTION
Speak to Sylvie to find out if she knows the impact, and state our expectations for an on-time start. Focus on need for everyone to start at same time because the rest of the plant depends on daily production. Give her an oral warning.
Help from?   no one
Refer to?   *no one*

Timing?   *Today*

WHEN I'LL CHECK RESULTS
Twice weekly follow-up with Sylvie regarding progress, for three weeks, then tapering off

Figure 10.3   Trevor's first try with the JR worksheet when Sylvie was late.

"For each option, ask yourself three questions:

1. Will this action strengthen or weaken the supervisory relationship with the individual?
2. Will this action strengthen or weaken the supervisory relationship with the group? And
3. Will this action improve or hurt production?

"If you just use a '+', a '0' or a '−' it gives you a very fast way to come up with the two or three most promising options. Why don't you give it a try."

I did. I was part way through and I marked one of the options as negative for the individual.

"Describe how you've come to that assessment," Julie interrupted.

I mentioned that Sylvie wouldn't like the option.

"Hmmm. Is the question whether Sylvie will like the action, or whether it will strengthen or weaken your supervisory relationship?"

I acknowledged that it was the second.

"Yes. We're not that interested about whether they like it. Of course, employees won't like discipline, if it comes to that. Or they won't like it when you say they can't leave early. But that's not the issue. It is whether they will respect you and acknowledge you as their boss, and do what you need, willingly and well."

"Oh. I get it. So Sylvie won't like me putting a note on her file, but the fact that I do will reinforce that I have specific expectations and she can't just ignore them when it's convenient for her."

"That's it."

Julie asked about how I'd have the conversation I was planning to have with her.

"Well I just thought I'd tell her that she'd been late again, and that wasn't OK and that I'm going to write her up."

"OK. But what action has she taken in that?"

"None, I guess."

"Has she made any commitments?"

"No."

"So that doesn't build her capacity. Does it fix the problem?"

I had to acknowledge that it didn't.

Julie carried on. "You need her to figure out her responsibility in this. Here's what I suggest. Start by stating that she was late yesterday by however long it was, and this is the second time this month, and then be quiet. Just wait for her to start talking. She will eventually. Just state the unacceptable behaviour – don't even comment on it. Just state it. And then wait.

"She'll probably give you a whole bunch of reasons. It doesn't matter what she says. And when she stops talking, you say, 'I hear what you've said. Regardless, being late isn't OK.' You can even give a short reason if you like. Then you ask, 'What are you going to do to fix it so you aren't late again?'

"Leave the problem with her. Then, when she has come up with a solution you're OK with, thank her for her commitment to fix the situation, and tell her that you will be giving her the written warning, and that you'll acknowledge what she is going to do to make sure it doesn't happen again."

I revised my plan (Figure 10.4) to account for this new thinking.

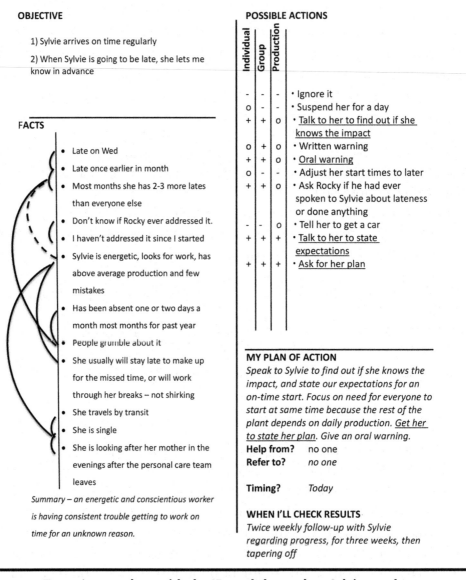

OBJECTIVE

1) Sylvie arrives on time regularly

2) When Sylvie is going to be late, she lets me know in advance

FACTS

- Late on Wed
- Late once earlier in month
- Most months she has 2-3 more lates than everyone else
- Don't know if Rocky ever addressed it.
- I haven't addressed it since I started
- Sylvie is energetic, looks for work, has above average production and few mistakes
- Has been absent one or two days a month most months for past year
- People grumble about it
- She usually will stay late to make up for the missed time, or will work through her breaks – not shirking
- She travels by transit
- She is single
- She is looking after her mother in the evenings after the personal care team leaves

Summary – an energetic and conscientious worker is having consistent trouble getting to work on time for an unknown reason.

POSSIBLE ACTIONS

Individual	Group	Production	
-	-	-	• Ignore it
o	-	-	• Suspend her for a day
+	+	o	• Talk to her to find out if she knows the impact
o	+	o	• Written warning
+	+	o	• Oral warning
o	-	-	• Adjust her start times to later
+	+	o	• Ask Rocky if he had ever spoken to Sylvie about lateness or done anything
-	-	o	• Tell her to get a car
+	+	+	• Talk to her to state expectations
+	+	+	• Ask for her plan

MY PLAN OF ACTION

Speak to Sylvie to find out if she knows the impact, and state our expectations for an on-time start. Focus on need for everyone to start at same time because the rest of the plant depends on daily production. Get her to state her plan. Give an oral warning.

Help from? no one

Refer to? no one

Timing? Today

WHEN I'LL CHECK RESULTS

Twice weekly follow-up with Sylvie regarding progress, for three weeks, then tapering off

Figure 10.4 Trevor's second try with the JR worksheet when Sylvie was late.

I went off to meet Sylvie and was amazed at the results. It was way more constructive than I'd expected, I suppose because the solution was Sylvie's idea. She is going to catch the next earlier bus. That will guarantee that she makes her connection. I left the conversation feeling quite upbeat.

Over the next four weeks there was no repeat. And because it was in my follow-up plan, I checked with her each week to see how it was going with her catching the earlier bus. She was pretty positive about it.

Over the next three months my hopes for the situation were more than rewarded. It was the first three-month period in which Sylvie hadn't had a late. I was delighted.

I knew I would use that card again.

Reflecting on the Chapter

For Supervisors (overseeing front-line workers)

- What are the recurring performance issues in your group? What has contributed to them going on for so long? What has the impact been on the group? What difference would it make if you could deal with some of them?
- How much of your time is currently consumed by dealing with performance issues?
- What unexpected reasons for poor performance do you think you might find if you spoke to people about their performance with curiosity, to get the facts, rather than going in with accusation?
- What would it be like in your department if the three biggest performance issues you faced went away? What would you spend your time on?
- How would the people you oversee react if those three big performance issues were resolved?
- What would it do to production if those three big performance issues were resolved?

Actions to Take

- The next time someone performs in a way that you don't like, try the approach of stating what they did, and that it is not OK, and then being silent. What happens? Wait for them to speak. When they have finished, restate that it is not OK, and ask them what they will do to fix it? What happens?
- Choose one of your team where you don't have the performance you need. Use the form to work through the situation and develop a plan. Make sure you can complete this checklist before you do anything else.
  - One objective for the mission of the organization, and one objective to look after your people
  - Gathered facts from:
    - The record
    - Spoken to the individual
    - Customs and rules from your workplace
    - Opinions and feelings
  - Eight possible actions listed

– A plan of action
– A plan for follow-up

Once you have it worked out this far, review the situation with your manager, then implement your plan.

■ Reflect on how it went when you applied this method.

For Managers *(you have supervisors or managers reporting to you)*

Consider all the questions for supervisors for yourself. Then consider the following.

■ How many performance issues are there among your direct reports that have not been dealt with over time? What has the impact been on the group and on the performance of their teams? What has contributed to them being ignored? What could you do that would change the situation?

■ How comfortable are you and the people who report to you with confronting poor performance? What has contributed to that reaction? Are there things you can do that would reduce any discomfort for the people that report to you?

Actions to Take

■ Share this chapter with a colleague, and then practice using the form with her/him so that you get comfortable using the method.

■ When the supervisors that report to you come to you with a performance problem, ask to see their completed form before you agree to do anything. If they don't have one, coach them through it, but make sure they do the work.

Chapter 11

The Accident

The phone call came at 7:06. I was fast asleep. I had planned to do an overnight hike with some friends and had taken the Friday off to do it. The plan for the day had been a leisurely morning doing some chores around the house, and then we were going to set off around 11 to drive to the trailhead.

I was actually feeling pretty good about how things were going. The training plan was working. Chrissy was working out extremely well. Sylvie's attendance issues had resolved. The improvement projects were proceeding well enough. The assembly department was getting the pieces they needed without a lot of expediting. As I had thought about taking a day off, I was thinking about Julie's expectation that I should be able to be away from the plant without the department skipping a beat. My Friday off was a little experiment.

I wasn't expecting the call to be from the plant. I remembered in my early days I couldn't even go out at lunch without getting phone calls. But now the people on my team were clear what to do next, so the phone calls stopped. I figured it was one of my eager buddies. I rolled over and picked up the phone.

"Yeah? What is it?" I growled. After the first few words I was completely awake.

An ambulance had been called. Katie, the first aid attendant was working to stop the blood flow. A couple of the guys had searched for and found Harry's fingers, and put them on ice. Now they were waiting.

"I'll be there in 25 minutes."

I dressed and was out the door in two minutes. No shave. I didn't even splash water on my face. It was hard to drive without speeding, without ignoring the rules, but in the back of my mind I knew that me getting in an accident wouldn't help.

Twenty-two minutes later I pulled into the plant. I was happy to see the ambulance crew wheeling Harry out to the waiting vehicle. He would be looked after for the moment. The team was standing around, looking somber and strained, shuffling from one foot to the other.

As I had driven in, I had been thinking about what my objectives were. Right back to Julie's lessons on Job Relations. I was so grateful for that tool.

I knew my first objective was to make sure everyone else was OK – emotionally as well as physically. I wanted to find out what happened, so we could prevent a repeat. And I had a niggling feeling that I'd need to look at safety more broadly, too.

I got out of my car and greeted the team. I walked over to Katie. "How are you holding up?"

"It was pretty scary," she started. She paused and I waited for her to go on. There'd be enough time to get the details. Now I just wanted to reassure her, and I knew the best way was to let her talk, and have all the emotions tumble out – as much as she wanted.

Over the next couple of minutes Katie described the sharp scream that filled the plant, the eerie silence in the moments after, punctuated by the hum of the exhaust fans, looking around to see what had happened and who was affected, her swift move to the medical aid room, her silent thanks that she'd gone over the contents of the kit two weeks ago, and her initial assessment of Harry.

A slight man, Harry joined the company three months before when he got tired of college and his cousin, Farah, suggested he apply. He'd done well. Katie found him sitting looking at his hand as blood pumped out of the second knuckle on two fingers with every heartbeat.

Katie cleared the floor and had him lie down. Blood loss was the challenge here. She took his hand, raised it up and squeezed the stumps of the fingers. The blood flow slowed.

She saw Sylvie standing there, and called to her. "I need four people. Get them here now." In fifteen seconds, Sylvie was back with three people in tow.

Katie had nodded at Teyjas. "Do you have a cell phone?" Teyjas nodded. "Good. Phone 911. Tell them there has been an industrial accident and the patient has lost fingers. Tell them there is a Level 2 First Aider. Give them our address. Tell me our address." Teyjas repeated it. "Good. Tell me when you have connected." In rapid succession she had given instructions to the others: one to get a blanket, one to keep talking to Harry, and one to head the search for the finger tips.

Instinctively, I knew that those four people plus the searchers would all need some time from me and maybe some other help, too.

Katie went on a bit more with details about the wait. They had found the fingers in five minutes and put them on ice. They were on their way to the hospital with Harry. Then she stopped. I could see her exhaustion.

"First off, thank you," I started. "You've done really well from what you've told me. You need a break. Take someone you're comfortable with and take half an hour. Go have a coffee or a short walk. I'll catch up with you then."

After giving Julie an update, I spent the next half hour speaking to everyone who had been in that part of the plant. What had they seen? What had they heard? What was going on at the time? By the end, I was pretty sure I knew the circumstances. I told them we'd keep everyone updated as best we could. But no one had seen it happen, so until I spoke to Harry I wouldn't know the exact sequence of events.

I headed back to the office and found Katie. "How are you doing?" She looked pale and exhausted. "Fine," she said in a clipped, controlled way, as if she were willing herself to stay composed. We exchanged a few more words.

"I think you need some rest, and you need to speak to someone about what happened." I paused. Katie was silent. "I have a couple of options for you. One is that I have a friend, Jess, who is with the ambulance service, so she'll know what you're going through. You can stay at work, and I'll see if she can come by for a chat. The second is that Mrs. K has just got us enrolled in that program where they have people who are really skilled at helping people through tough moments. You can use Mrs. K's room – I know she won't be in today – and call them. Whichever you choose is fine. Or maybe you've got another idea. Do you want a couple of minutes to decide?"

Katie shook her head. "No," she started. "Call your friend. See if she can come."

I dialled. Jess answered and I breathed a sigh of relief. Even better, she could come by within the hour. I let Katie know.

Then I went to do my own investigation of the accident scene. I was just about finished when, 20 minutes later, Katie came by. She looked better, less strained. A few words with her and I decided it would be okay for her to go back to work until Jess came by, as long as it was a minor task that didn't require much attention.

Next, I needed to do two things. Rounds to get everyone's mind back on their work. And I knew I needed to review safety protocols.

I did my rounds, checking on each person on the team. Did they know what was next up? Did they have everything they needed to finish their current task? When did they think they'd finish it? Had they encountered any obstacles? And, had there been any safety concerns? I winced at the irony of that question.

I attended to the two matters that came up. Zhou had had more pieces split than usual and was going to be 23 pieces short for her current lot. I did a couple of tests and asked a couple of questions. It became clear that this wood was drier than usual. I added that to my longer-term list of things to sort out.

Chrissy had seen some tearing in the holes she was drilling. A quick check, and a question or two and it became clear that she hadn't mastered how to check the sharpness of her bits. I lined up Sunil to train her that afternoon.

At that point, I knew I needed to address the safety issue, but I wasn't sure how. I knew Julie would help, but she'd be expecting me to have done some homework. After a bit of internet research, I realized that the place to start was with the company's own experience.

Late in the morning I spoke to Neil and asked him for the company's safety and WCB records over the past three years. Neil asked if I'd like the averages for their industry. "I didn't even know you could get that."

"Oh yes," Neil replied. "Workers' Comp is really keen to drive down the injury rate so they have a ton of information available. We're paying a pretty hefty premium right now. We spend over $80,000 a year, and we could probably save half that if we could match the best in our industry. And that's not counting all the other costs."

"What do you mean – 'other costs'?"

"Well, Workers' Comp figures that their premiums are less than a third of the total cost of accidents. There is the downtime – like the time you're spending now. And the lost production. And the lost productivity for the next few days as people think about the accident. And it goes on. They estimate even minor accidents can cost literally thousands of dollars."

"I had no idea." I finished up the conversation and headed back to my area. Along the way I swung by Julie's office. There was no sign of her, so I scribbled a short note.

Then I went to the first aid logbook and sat down to go over it. At first I didn't really know what to look for, but by the time I had scanned the first aid reports for the last three months I had some ideas. Thirty-five reports in the last 90 days. Mostly small, but there they were. And really concentrated in two areas of the plant: my department and shipping. I also noticed that 21 of the 35 were the same three people. One was Harry – this was his 10th incident – but his 6th on the same machine that he had been hurt on. Another was Zhou. Hers wasn't concentrated on one machine, but there were lots of small cuts. I needed to follow up with both of them. And then one of the people in shipping.

That gave me enough for a conversation with Julie. I knew where I wanted to start. Monday I would spend some time watching the machine run, and then I'd have a close look at the machine itself. I went back to Neil to get the forms I needed to file, finished them up for Julie's signature and went to find her.

Julie listened to my summary. "I have to say that I'm pretty happy with how you handled this, especially for someone who hasn't dealt with this stuff before. So let's go back to the Job Relations process again. Have you covered it all off?"

"Job Relations?" I asked. "This is about safety, not Job Relations!"

"Yes and no," she countered. "Think about it, and come and see me when you have some ideas. I've seen you do lots of problem solving. You can think this through yourself. Come see me on Monday and let me know what you've come up with and where you're stuck. In the meantime, get out of here. This was supposed to be a day off for you. I'll do your rounds for you after the lunch break. You've done what you need to. Go catch up with your buddies and have a good hike. I still don't see what's to like about lugging a pack up and down mosquito-infested trails." She shook her head in mock disgust. "The only camping I want to do is at a resort." Then she waved me off.

I left with a mix of emotions. I was pretty pleased that Julie seemed to have such confidence in my abilities. But I sure didn't feel very confident about it.

The rest of that day I had Julie's question rolling around in the back of my head. How did Job Relations method connect with safety? I just couldn't see it. After all, I didn't think I had any bad actors, and I couldn't imagine any of my crew wanting to injure themselves.

That evening I was mulling it over as I lay in my sleeping bag. I decided I might as well go back to the simple form Julie had introduced me to four months ago. I started filling it out in my mind. By the time I was done, I got what Julie was pointing at. The Job Relations model gave me a nice structured way to look at what was happening, even when it wasn't exactly related to the performance of particular individuals. I realized that it was really a problem-solving tool. We had just always used it for people-related problems. When I got back from the hike I put it down on paper (Figure 11.1). I had a plan to present to Julie.

On Monday, I sat down with Julie and walked her through the worksheet, including my plan. I'd underlined the actions I'd decided to do. "Nicely

OBJECTIVE

1) Everyone goes home intact at the end of every day and no close calls

2) Increase productivity

FACTS

- Harry had cut off parts of two fingers
- 25 accidents in last 3 months (one every 3 days)
- Don't know if it is a trend
- 16 from just two people, Harry and Zhou, and 3 from Sylvie
- 10 in shipping, 12 in parts, remaining ones scattered
- One in my department (Chrissy) is new to our plant - 2 incidents
- Harry is new to woodworking
- 11 were from two machines, including 6 from the machine Harry was using
- There was no safety program in the company other than a ten-minute intro when people started
- Most of the machines aren't guarded, including the two problem ones
- I ask if people have safety concerns during my rounds, but I've never had any raised
- Katie is a really good first aider, from what I can tell

POSSIBLE ACTIONS

Individual	Group	Production	
o	+	o	• Find out if there is a trend
+	+	o	• Ask Katie what trends or patterns she has seen
o	+	-	• Guard all the machines
o	o	o	• Create a safety program
			• Fire the people who have accidents
			• Discipline anyone who has an accident
+	+	o	• Ask employees what is dangerous
-	o	o	• Hire a consultant to tell us what to do
+	+	o	• Ask Harry what happened
+	+	o	• Ask the last five people injured what happened to find a pattern
-	-	-	• Do nothing and hope
+	+	+	• Ask people how the job could be safer and faster or easier

MY PLAN OF ACTION

Check if there is trend over time.
Ask operators how job could be safer, faster, or easier. From that I'll create a specific improvement plan
Help from? *Julie, Jamie, operators*
Refer to? *no one*

Timing? *1 week to get all input, 1 week to define the rest of the program*
WHEN I'LL CHECK RESULTS
Weekly follow-up with Julie

Figure 11.1 Trevor's JR worksheet for addressing the accident rate at Sussex Creek Boatworks.

done, Trevor," she started. "I have just a couple of comments. First, I think you need to include guarding the machines, regardless of how effective you think that will be. Guards don't make up for 'stupid', but if we looked at the workplace safety regulations, you'd find that appropriate guards are required. Are you familiar with the hierarchy of hazard controls?"

I shook my head.

"I'm not surprised. You'd never have had a reason to run across it. Basically, it says that you address safety issues in the following sequence." She went to her whiteboard, and wrote (Table 11.1):

Table 11.1 Hierarchy of Safety Controls

1. Eliminate – Design it out
2. Substitute – Use something else
3. Engineering Controls – technology and design, isolation and guarding
4. Administrative Controls – procedures, training, policy
5. Personal Protective Equipment – last resort

As she wrote, she described each one – how the further down the list you go, the more likely that human error can cause the method to fail and result in injury.

"You can see," she concluded, "that really we want to eliminate hazards where we can, and we want to use a solution that relies as little as possible on people remembering stuff.

"Second, I notice that one of the facts is that there is no safety program. Maybe you had this in mind, but I know that there isn't any systematic training for using each machine, so the basic safety matters that should be built into that training aren't being covered off. That's a big hole.

"As long as you keep those two things in mind – the hierarchy of control, and building key points about safety matters into our Job Instruction breakdowns – we should be OK. So, follow your plan. You'll find lots of opportunities. What I'd like you to do as well is find someone who knows about guarding and get them in to help us. There is a lot that someone good can teach us in minutes that would take us years to figure out, so although it wasn't in the budget for this year, we'll find the funds for this. We don't want a repeat of what happened with Harry. I'll text you the contact info for a couple of people that might be able to help. They won't be the people we need, but they'll probably know someone local who is good at this stuff." She scrolled through her contacts list and texted me a couple.

A bit of small talk, and then I turned to go. I had just stepped out of Julie's door when I turned back. "OK," I said, smiling. "I think I'm starting to figure some of this stuff out. What's the priority for this safety stuff? We're trying to get our production rates up another 10% in the next three months, and my plate's pretty full as it is. When should this be completed?"

Julie smiled back at me. "Three days ago would have been good, because then Harry wouldn't have been hurt. But since that's not possible, can we get this done in a month?"

I stared at her, mouth open. "A month? With everything else?"

"Yup," Julie said. "We have to look after our people, and we have to look after the business. Both are critical. And in this case, I think you'll find that as you make things safer, you'll improve productivity. We'll have our cake and eat it too. And, so you can do some planning... anything up to $500 per machine, you have my authority to proceed. If it is more than that, I'd like to know what you're proposing to do. By the way, do you want a hint?"

"Sure." Why would I say "no"?

"OK." Julie almost seemed to be purring, she was so pleased. "Four things. First, if you have a look at the detailed sheets from your Job Improvement efforts, it will let you see quickly where the risks are, and if you go through the questions and add the question, 'How can the risk be reduced?' then you'll get lots of good ideas."

"Second. Don't try to do this on your own. There's too much to do, and as you've seen with the Job Improvement process, when you involve your team you get way better results. Third, try to make it fun. Safety is a really serious matter, but we don't have to be serious while we work on it. See what you can do to make it fun.

"Finally, you know there are two machines that are a problem right away. You and Sunil need to develop some training that will address the risks of those machines, and get everyone who uses them trained by the end of this week. The key points have to incorporate the elements of how to do the task so it is safe. They'll be part of the Job Instruction Breakdown sheet. Of course, guarding is a better solution than just instructions, but you won't get the guards in place that fast. You can have the instruction completed in a day or two."

"Oh, yes. One other thing. There is always one other thing, isn't there? Although I'm leaving you with the job of doing this in your area, I'm going to be pushing this to the other supervisors, too. Shipping needs some work, as you've seen, and so does Finishing. Your review showed us that."

I left Julie's office shaking my head. I was always amazed at the deadlines Julie put on tasks. One month, with everything else that is going on? And then I remembered her advice. Of course! If I was going to do it all on my own, there is no way I could get it done. But if I enlisted the help of my team, I could stay focused on a few key things – like getting the consultant lined up.

*****

Three weeks later, I was having a conversation with Julie. "I don't think I will hit your one-month target, but we'll be close. We finally got the consultant in last week, and she walked through the shop. She had ideas for just about every operation. Mostly the people on the team think they will work, but there are a couple that clearly need some more thought." I paused. "Are experts and consultants really so clueless about how things work in the real world?"

"Not always." Julie laughed. "But when you realize that she had only spent 3 hours in the plant, it's not a surprise that she doesn't understand the whole range of our production. Just think what it's like for our new staff. We focus them on core tasks first, and then later we introduce them to the weird stuff we do. She's the same. We'll take what we can use. And we can always go back and ask questions later."

"Anyway," I went on, "we know what we need on the six machines where over 95 percent of the accidents happen. From what the vendor tells me, we'll have the appropriate guards in place by the end of next week. And we've spoken to each of the operators to get their take on the risks at each machine, and apart from one at the router, we have solutions for everything."

"Great," Julie replied. "Did you ever work out whether there was a longer-term trend in our injury pattern?"

"Funny you should ask," I responded. "There was a trend, but not what I'd expected. The last 90 days was better than a year ago, which I know is pretty shocking. So, things seemed to start changing around the time Rocky left."

"I'm not surprised," she commented. "Disappointed but not surprised. I've seen it before where changing one person in the leadership team makes a huge difference to the safety of everyone. We won't make a big deal about it. We'll just focus everyone on getting to zero injuries, regardless of where we start. It won't happen without some effort! What do you need me to do to help you?"

"When you're ready," I started, "I want you to come and speak to one of my morning stand up meetings. I know you're trying to get this going in the other parts of the company, too, so if you want to coordinate across the departments, I get that. But we're steaming ahead, and I'd like you to reinforce the message."

"I can do that," Julie responded. "I won't wait for the others, so let me know when you want me there."

"Today is Thursday. Month end is on the weekend. How about Monday morning? New month. Renewed focus on safety. We'll have lots to celebrate because we've had a great month with best productivity ever, and only three late deliveries to the rest of the plant. This will just add to the direction."

"That sounds like a great plan," Julie commented. "I'll see you Monday morning at 8:20 for the 8:30 huddle."

"See you then," I replied. I was about to head back to the plant, when I turned back. "Have you heard how Harry is doing?" I asked.

Julie shook her head. "Not today. I talked to Farah yesterday. She said that the fingers had been reattached and were working really well. Harry's got it in his mind that he's going to be playing the sitar again within six months. He was so lucky they were severed so cleanly."

"Thanks for the update," I smiled. "That's a real relief to hear. The crew have been asking." Julie seemed to let out a breath, as if she'd been holding it forever. I headed back to the plant.

I felt very good about how things were going. Just the fact that I was looking at safety seemed to have made a difference. There had only been five first-aid incidents in the plant so far that month, whereas in the months before there'd have been twice as many. It was a good start. The investigations I was doing after each incident kept pointing to the same risk areas. As we learned about the risks, we kept revising our Job Instruction Breakdowns to incorporate the new information about key points related to safety. I felt confident that we would be picking off the worst of the hazards.

Reflecting on the Chapter

For Supervisors (overseeing front line workers)

- Where do accidents repeat in your workplace? What about close calls?
- How much production do you lose when there is a safety incident or accident? Try to think of all the people involved.

Actions to Take

- Read through the accident and incident reports for your area over the past six months and look for patterns.[1]
- If your company has a designated safety person, speak to them, and ask them to walk with you through your area without turning it into an audit. Ask for their help to learn how to see the risks that are there. For each risk, ask the person how many actual incidents have happened from that risk, so you can make your own assessment about priority.
- If you don't have a safety officer, ask one of your more thoughtful employees to walk with you through your area to look for risks. Use the results of your review as a jumping-off point.
- Identify two or three risks that you would like to deal with in your area over the next month.

For Managers (you have supervisors or managers reporting to you)

Consider all the questions for supervisors yourself. Then consider the following.

- When was the last time you asked any of the people reporting to you how safety was in their area?
- Is safety a topic in any of the meetings you hold? How about any of the meetings you go to?

---

[1] Each jurisdiction has different labels for injury events. The labels can include reportable incidents, first aid only, medical aid, clinic visits, accidents, lost-time accidents, near-misses, and so on. If you're not sure about the terms used in your area, ask the person who files the injury reports for your company, or look on the website of the organization that provides workplace insurance to your company.

Actions to Take

- On your next walk through each of your areas, ask each person you speak with about their observations about safety in their area.
- In future, make a point as you speak to people in your area to ask about safety issues. When did they feel they were doing something with higher-than-normal risk?
- Incorporate safety into every meeting of the people that report to you. One option is to start each meeting with one minute for safety in which you review a recent initiative, or discuss a recent incident, or report out on safety performance, so safety is front of mind for your team. Alternatively, you can include a safety oriented agenda item in each meeting.

Chapter 12

Ship Collisions and Failing Funnels

Late in the day, Terri, who looked after our shipping, came hustling up to me.

"I couldn't find anyone else to help me," she started. Gil, her boss, had already gone for the day. She had a fellow from Stupendous Gifts on the line, "angrier than a nest of riled up hornets," she related. They had received our last shipment and they weren't happy. "They want to know what we plan to do," she concluded.

I still wasn't clear what the problem was. "Is Julie around?" I asked. I was going to handle the situation but normally shipping wasn't part of my area of responsibility, and I didn't want to step on anyone's toes.

"You're the only one in management I could find," Terri responded.

"What's his name?" I gestured at the phone with the blinking light.

"Troy."

I picked up the phone, wondering how this was going to play out.

Fifteen minutes later I hung up the phone with a plan that Troy had grudgingly agreed to. The last shipment of 50 toy boats had arrived. Half of them had no funnels attached. They were in the box alright, but they had come loose. To make matters worse, many of the toys had dents in the ends and sides where they had clearly banged into each other during the voyage – I mean, the shipment. Troy was annoyed because he had customers who wanted these items, and he couldn't deliver, and doubly annoyed because, as he had told me, "this is not the first or second time this has happened."

I reflected how the same skills I'd learned from Julie about dealing with my employees worked really well with customers too. I made a mental note to say thank you to her.

I'd agreed to let him know by tomorrow how fast we could get a shipment to him, and told him that we'd change our gluing process and our packaging to fix those issues.

The next morning at the supervisor's stand-up meeting I talked about the call and asked for help from Gil.

Julie listened to everything. Then she started. "I'm interested that Troy said this was not the first time this has happened to him. What other shipments have we heard about?"

Gil shook his head. "This is the first time I've heard about it. I had no idea. Not from him or anyone."

And I volunteered that I hadn't noticed anything. We just made the boats we had orders for, but we'd had no feedback about glue issues or funnels.

Julie picked up the discussion. "So we have a situation that in our customer's mind is a repeated problem, that we've fixed before, but none of the supervisors know about it. How is that possible?"

We all looked at each other, a bit sheepishly.

Julie paused. "I actually need to correct myself and apologize. Asking 'How is that possible' isn't very constructive and has more blame in it than I'd like. We have a current condition – sort of. And we probably have a target condition we need to reach that hasn't been stated clearly. So, Gil, Peter and Trevor, can you please come back to us tomorrow with a clear statement of the current condition, our target condition, the obstacles that would prevent us from reaching that target, and your suggestion about which one to tackle first?"

We nodded, and the meeting moved on.

I thought about what would have happened under Rocky. He'd have exploded, we'd have all scurried away, he'd have imposed a solution without really understanding the situation, and we'd all go on, but the problem might still linger on, causing further explosions.

Later that day Gil, Peter and I met and worked out what we thought was the route to go. I was pretty pleased because we got it done in about 25 minutes; I'd been expecting it to take most of an hour. But by now Julie had gotten all of us used to problem solving rather than blaming, so we stayed focused on what might be happening, rather than whose fault it was.

By the end of the day I got back to Troy. I didn't have a fix worked out, so I told him that I'd personally baby the order through the plant and that we figured we'd have new processes in place within a couple of weeks. In the meantime, we'd do some extra inspection. He was grudgingly OK with that. Then on a whim I asked him to take pictures of the funnel holes for half a dozen of the boats. And we worked out that he'd ship all but ten back to us, and that he'd glue the funnels in those ten himself. I checked that he had the right sort of glue, and we hung up.

Next morning, we presented our plan to Julie. We just hung around after the stand-up meeting and dealt with it.

What came up from our initial exploration was that we didn't really understand what was happening – the current condition. Gil had done some observations in the packaging area and Peter and I had spent some time observing the gluing area. I'd got Yvonne from Sales to pull out the customer complaint histories to see if she could find out how often this was happening. It turned out to be every week or so we'd have a problem, and it seemed to inconsistently affect the production for a day or two.

We suspected we had two problems and one was exposing the other. The packaging wasn't solid, and then when it wasn't solid, the boats would bang around and the collisions would knock off the funnels. At least that was our hypothesis – our best explanation. But we weren't sure.

We decided that Gil would tackle the packaging issue, and Peter and I would deal with the glue problem.

Our priority was to fix the packaging issue, since that's what the customer saw right away. Gil figured that his challenge was to have every boat arrive in exactly the shape it was when it was shipped. He'd also set his first target condition – demonstrate a packing method that eliminated collisions. Then he listed the obstacles he'd come up with.

- A single large cavity in the box
- Variation in the orders – not always the same combinations of boats in the box
- Variation in how the boats are wrapped
- Variation in how tightly the boats are fitted into the boxes
- Some wrapped in paper, and some in foam
- No standards for wrapping – left to shipper to decide
- We don't know how things survive when we wrap them a particular way
- We have inconsistency in who does the wrapping – Terri plus whoever can help her at the time

Gil actually got pretty excited as he led us through his list. "I had no idea we had so many opportunities," he exclaimed. After a few minutes of discussion, Gil decided to embark on a week of experiments, shipping products to a store 22 hours away by road. Julie gave him some help designing the experiments so he only needed to send out about 20 packages to get the results he needed. Gil figured he'd have some initial results in a couple of days, and everything wrapped up in a week. He laughed at his own pun as he said it.

Peter and I had a challenge on our hands. Why was the problem so inconsistent? We were just gluing funnels and pushing them into holes. Not complicated. At least it didn't seem that way to us. We decided to go and watch. I guess Julie's insistence to "go see" was starting to have an influence on us both.

An hour later we were stunned at what we'd seen. We'd watched three different people do the task and seen three completely different techniques. One dropped a dollop of glue in the bottom and pushed the funnel in. One had coated the bottom part of the funnel, pushed it in and wiped off the excess glue, and one had coated the inside of the hole, and shoved in the funnel. And we'd seen each of them struggle to get the funnels to fit, but it was inconsistent; some went in easily.

We had no idea which was best or which method was giving us the problems.

So now we had identified our own challenge – we wanted funnels to never come out of their holes, and we knew a bit about the current situation – inconsistent processes and weekly reports of failures. We developed our own list of obstacles that we thought were preventing us reaching our target.

- Not a consistent way to apply glue
- Variety of people doing the work
- Operators use different amounts of glue
- Don't know which approach is better
- Operators have to struggle to fit some funnels

It took us a while to agree on our next target condition. We decided that if we could stabilize on one process that would be a good first step. Then we'd see what else was needed to achieve our challenge. But which one?

Our most important obstacle to making improvements was that we didn't know which method worked and which one was the problem. So that became our first task. We had to do some testing to see which methods worked. I guess Julie's insistence on doing experiments was starting to rub off on us. Peter and I worked out a test program. Glue fifteen funnels each way, let them set for a day, and then see how much force was needed to pull out the funnels. And we got clever… we asked the three different people to insert the funnels the way they usually did, with no other instruction, and just kept an eye on them to make sure they did it the way we expected. They did. People are such creatures of habit.

Two days later we were expecting an easy answer. One or two of the methods would be fine, we figured, and one would prove to be a problem. Instead, we found that about 20 percent of the funnels popped free without difficulty in the ones with the dollop of glue, while about a third popped free from the other two methods.

Despite being sure that it was how the gluing was being done, the testing proved to us that we'd guessed wrong about the most important obstacle. But we'd learned something. It wasn't the glue. And we were back to square one. We still didn't know why some funnels were solidly glued and others weren't. We brought this back to our stand-up meeting.

"How consistent are the funnels?" Sally asked.

"What do you mean?" Peter responded.

"I just remember at another company I worked, where we were gluing, we found that the dimensions really mattered. It wasn't wood. It was plastic. But we found that if there was too big a gap between the piece and the hole, we wouldn't get the contact we needed, and the glue joints would fail. Could that be a problem with wood, too?"

And then it was like a lightbulb went on for Peter. "Hey," he turned to me. "Remember we saw some of the operators had real trouble inserting the funnels, and some went in really easily…? Maybe there is enough variation to make a difference!"

"Thanks, Sally. That gives us something to work on. It sure is the most promising possibility."

That afternoon Peter and I spent 20 minutes with the digital callipers. We'd charted out the diameters in two directions on 50 parts. The charts told their own story (Figure 12.1). The funnels weren't circular, they were oval. Not a lot – not so the eye would notice – but maybe it was enough. Certainly, if the short dimension was at the short end of the tolerance it didn't touch the sides of the hole. And it seemed that if the long dimension was on the short end of our tolerances, then the funnels were very loose. Now we had something to test.

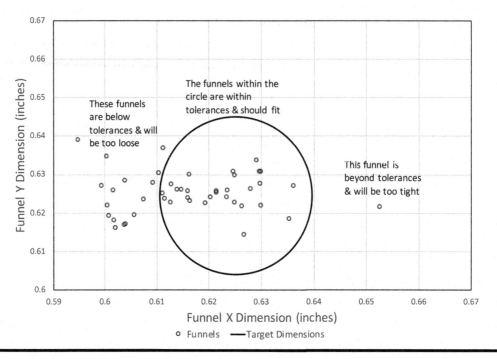

Figure 12.1 Plot of measured cross section dimensions for 50 funnels.

We got Sylvie to drill 50 test holes into a plank, and then glued in 50 parts, keeping track of the dimensions. The next day we did our test pulls and confirmed our hypothesis. When the long-side dimension was at the short end of the range, the glue didn't hold. Just to be sure, we got the team to run another set of tests using the three different gluing methods on parts we thought would work. They all held just fine. So, although there was no standard way of applying the glue, it didn't matter as long as the dimensions were good. We had learned something.

Now we needed to go back to look at the source of the parts.

Before the end of the day I phoned Troy, our irate customer. I told him what we'd done and what we'd found.

"You did what?" he asked, sounding incredulous! "You did all that testing just because I groused?"

"No, Troy. We didn't do it because you groused. We did it because that is how we get better. We just follow this process that Julie, our operations manager taught us, and it seems to make a difference in the results we get. We haven't figured out how to stop making the badly sized parts yet, but at least we know not to use them, and tomorrow I'm going to make a little go/no-go jig so they're easy to test."

"A what? A gogo jig? What does gogo dancing have to do with it? Gogo was something from the 60s – last century. You weren't even born."

"Just barely born in the last century, Troy. What I meant was that I'll make a jig – a little tool – that the operator can use to test whether or not the part has the correct dimensions. If it meets the requirements, it's a 'Go,' and if it fails, it's a 'No Go' (Figure 12.2). We'll design it so it is a single operation. It should take us about 20 minutes to make it, and it will take about 10 seconds, tops, to test each funnel just before it is glued in. And if I'm doing my job right, within a week or two we'll have figured out how to prevent us making them wrong in the first place and we won't even need the jig. We do all that, and we're going to eliminate your problems of funnels falling out, and we might even improve our costs."

"I'll be looking for a price reduction, then!" Troy quipped.

"I don't think there will be enough from this to make anything noticeable on the price, but you can take that up with your sales rep."

"Well, you've got me curious," Troy went on. "Any chance I could come over and see what you're doing the next time I'm in town?"

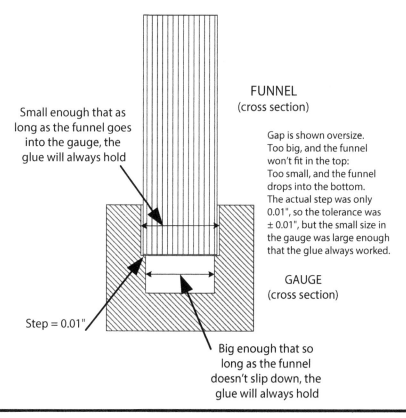

FUNNEL
(cross section)

Small enough that as long as the funnel goes into the gauge, the glue will always hold

Gap is shown oversize. Too big, and the funnel won't fit in the top: Too small, and the funnel drops into the bottom. The actual step was only 0.01", so the tolerance was ± 0.01", but the small size in the gauge was large enough that the glue always worked.

GAUGE
(cross section)

Step = 0.01"

Big enough that so long as the funnel doesn't slip down, the glue will always hold

Figure 12.2 Sketched cross section of Trevor's go/no-go gauge.

"I can check with Julie," I replied, "but I don't see why not. I'll ask her to give you a call."

With that, we said our goodbyes, and I hung up the phone.

***

The go/no-go gauge was ready that afternoon, and worked like a charm. We just made it from some scrap hardwood. I suppose if it was going to be a longer-term solution, we'd have used steel, but we figured it would be a couple of weeks at most. We pulled together the important steps, key points and reasons for how to use it and trained the people doing the gluing. It was pretty quick and informal, but it worked, and as Peter checked over the next couple of days, we never saw anyone make a mistake.

While we'd been working on the gluing problem, Gil and Terri had been working on the packaging issue. They'd come up with a solution that they'd proven by shipping some boats across the country and back. The new approach was a bit faster to package, but it used more expensive materials, so Gil was going to continue to work with his team to reduce the cost. But we knew the boats would arrive intact. Gil and Terri had worked out that shipping one boat back to us wound up costing about $125, for everyone's time, and the shipping, and the replacement boat and the inspection and the paperwork. We could afford a few extra cents per boat in the short term to prevent the damage.

Meantime, Peter and I carried on with our efforts to find out why we were getting funnels with an oval shape, and what we could do to correct it. We went to the moulder and watched. Again, we saw so many possible reasons, but again, we started by getting clear on our challenge: We wanted every funnel we produced to meet our dimensional requirements. And we knew our current condition: 30 percent of pieces were too oval to glue properly.

Our first insight was that if we gave a go/no-go gauge to the person running the moulder, we could do the test once at each set-up and then check every length that ran through the machine. That way, we'd know that every funnel we cut from that length would be fine. Then the folks doing assembly wouldn't have to check – ever.

Then we built our starting obstacle list. We got the best ideas from Teyjas and Sunil, who ran the moulder. In half an hour we had our list, and had picked an obstacle to start working on.

- Sharpening process for knives elongates the shape
- Moulder will run even when heads not aligned properly

- Knives tricky to set into moulder consistently
- Debris build-up in the guides results in the dowel being a bit off-centre
- Hard to get the head location "just right," so operators get "close enough" and stop adjusting

Over the next 15 days we worked our way through the details of this problem. Every day we'd look at what we learned, see if we were at our target condition, rethink the obstacles, and work out the next experiment. By the time we finished we'd done several things:

1. A go/no-go jig for the knives made sure they were correct before they were mounted;
2. An index tool made it easier to have the two heads properly aligned. It reduced our set-up time by 10 minutes, too;
3. We added a specially shaped guide to keep the alignment of the dowel correct between the heads; and
4. We worked out a Job Instruction for the change-over of the moulder that had the key points needed to get the job done correctly, and retrained the operators.

From then on, we were fine. The funnels fit. We never had another one come loose. And Gil and his team eventually found a source for box dividers that were basically free: they were the off-cuts from a box maker who was only too happy to reduce his scrap.

***

A month later I got a call from Troy.

"I'm going to be in town next Tuesday. Do you have time for me to visit?" No greeting. No introduction. Just gruff Troy. Just like him.

"Sure," I responded. "What do you want to see?"

"I want to see what you guys do so that you solve a problem like that in a month, and reduce your costs at the same time. I just don't get it."

"Then I think you should plan on being at the plant when I start at 6:50."

"What?" he barked? "What civilized manager starts then? That's when the employees start."

"Yup. And that's when I start: actually, I'm here before that. My general manager is often here at that time, too." I thought I'd put in a dig here, and brag about our GM. I didn't like the way he separated himself from his people. "Be here. And bring me a coffee for my troubles. One sugar, one milk. Large." If he could be gruff, I could give it right back. "See you at 6:50. Don't be late. I'll have a crew of eight ready to work and I can't wait for you."

I hung up.

I was actually pretty pumped. Troy was a hard guy to please. But here he was, giving us the only compliment he knew how to. He was bringing his skeptical self to our plant to see how we did it.

I told the team at the next morning's stand-up meeting. We all grinned and there were high-five's all around. After the stand-up meeting I cornered Julie.

"You know we'd never have managed this a year ago. Thank you."

"We're just getting started, Trevor." She smiled back at me. "Up 'til now, I've been able to draw on my experience to give you guidance. But now I'm reaching the threshold of my knowledge, and we're going to be learning together."

***

Next Tuesday I was at the plant a bit early, because I wanted to be there well ahead of Troy. Just because he was here didn't mean I could avoid my morning tasks, and I didn't need him reading over my shoulder as I scanned the notes from the end of yesterday's shift.

At 6:45 Troy drove into the parking lot. He had my coffee – and had it right. Then I saw something that pushed him up a notch in my eyes. He had brought boxes of donuts – enough for everyone at the plant, with leftovers.

"Good morning to you," I beamed. "So glad you could make it. Welcome to Sussex Creek Boatworks."

"Morning'," he responded. "I don't remember when I last got to a plant this early."

"We can chat a bit later." I checked that he was outfitted with the right safety gear, and then started walking, motioning him to follow me. "Right now, we need to get to the morning huddle. It's how the team starts every day. I just spent the last 10 minutes getting ready for it, though good-ness knows it's way easier now than it was when we started. Anyway, I'll introduce you to the team and then what I'd ask is that you just watch and listen. When we're finished, I'll ask a couple of our senior folks to stay on for a few minutes and you can ask any questions you want. I'll leave you with them while I attend to a couple of things. Everyone here knows we don't tell people about our costs, but anything else is fair game. Once I'm back, I'll take you around to meet some of the others, especially Gil and Terri in shipping. Any questions?"

"You're all business for 6:45 in the morning. Yeah, I got it. I'll watch and listen." We were approaching the huddle board.

"Morning everyone," I said as we arrived. "I'd like you to meet Troy. He's the customer from Stupendous Gifts who was so helpful in identifying the funnel problem. He got curious about how we fixed the problem so quickly. He asked if he could come and see. I checked with Julie and she said OK. So he's a guest. Usual rules apply. Please make him welcome and feel free to answer any questions within our company limits."

"Jas, you're leading today, are you?" I turned to Jas.

"Yup," she replied. "Ok everyone. Welcome to Tuesday. How do you know it's Toosday?" There was silence. "Because it's not Onesday."

Everyone laughed and ribbed her about the lame joke.

"Just trying to keep up the standards," Jas quipped. "Five great things from yesterday." She was all business.

The team piped up.

"No accidents or near misses."

"We got that rush order done two hours before pick-up time so we didn't have to drive it to the terminal."

"The experiment we ran yesterday with the hull jig didn't work but we figured out why and have the next experiment designed."

"I heard that the new Lake Winnipeg fishboat design was accepted by the Manitoba Tourist Association."

"The new guy in the paint shop, Tam? He finished his training a day ahead and is working right at standard."

"Thanks everyone," Jas said. "Here's the rundown. Yesterday we had orders for parts for 625 boats and we produced parts for 645. The 20 extra were catch up from Friday when we had the machine issue. One batch of 32 was 60 minutes late to assembly. Marcus and I will be looking at why after the meeting. That's the first late batch in three weeks. All the machines ran without issue, except the chop saw. It's been running with a one-half a degree angle error for four days now. Jamie knows about it and her current projection is it will be fixed on Thursday when a part comes in. Productivity was at 103 percent of standard, and our five-day average is on standard. All in all, we're on track, other than that late batch and the chop saw. Giles?"

"No safety issues," piped up Giles, who is the safety person on our team. "We're now at 27 days with no incidents or lost time accidents."

Jas led us through the other agenda items: priorities for the day, who was going to need help, what training was happening and what experiments were going to happen.

She turned to me. "Company news, Trevor?"

"Thanks Jas. The only company news has already been mentioned. That new Lake Winnipeg Fishboat is now an official product. In the next week we'll be doing training for all the parts. Our target is to be ready for orders in two weeks. We think it will sell probably 500–700 units per year, and the Lake Winnipeg boats are quite similar to the local fishing boats in two other regions so we may be able to adjust the design for those markets."

"Thanks, Trevor," Jas said. She wrapped up.

We were done in 12 minutes. The crew headed off to their work. Jas and Sunil stayed behind. "We can answer any questions you have now, Troy," I started. "I'll leave you with Jas and Sunil, and I'll be back in about five minutes." I went off to follow up on a couple of items, and headed back in five minutes.

Troy asked a lot of questions. A couple of times he asked about costs and we reminded him that we don't discuss costs with folks outside the company. He was amazed that we did our stand-up meeting every day. "When we do stand-up meetings, we all get same message. No-one has to repeat talking to everyone," said Sunil. "Save 15 minutes. All hear same message. Everyone same same. More time for making things better or fixing things or training."

When Troy was finished with his questions, I took him over to where Peter and I were working on another of our improvement projects. I explained that when we'd fixed the funnel situation, we'd seen a lot of variation in the moulder operation, and we'd got curious about whether it was affecting other parts. I showed him the jigs and the go/no-go gauge that we'd created. We'd found out that the head alignment issue was affecting most of the moulder parts, increasing our sanding time. We figured we could take a minute out of most of our boats by fixing that. As we were talking, Julie came by. I introduced her.

"How did you figure all this out?" he asked.

"We didn't. Julie brought this with her. We've been at it for six months or so now – we do something most days. Oh, yeah, there are a few exceptions, but I bet it's no more than once a week." I looked questioning at Julie. She nodded her head. "And it's every supervisor in the plant, so we're getting some stuff done."

We talked about how we got started and I described how it had been six months before Julie even started to introduce this. I talked about learning the Job Instruction and Job Relations skills, and what a difference that had made for me.

With that, I thanked Troy for the coffee and the donuts, and excused myself.

Julie told me later that Troy had been very impressed, and said he was going to look at using something like these methods in his operation. Then she laughed. "Just like so many business people, he thinks his operation is different and special, and our methods probably won't work. But he's intrigued enough to try it." She shook her head. "I don't get how so many smart people think their business is unique or different enough that good, proven methods won't work. I guess it's just that they've never seen it work in their industry, and they're fundamentally risk-averse. Anyway, I wished him well. We know this approach works, and I hope you see that it doesn't matter what industry you're in."

"Oh yes," I responded emphatically. "I can see that. Do you think it will work for him?"

"I'll reserve judgment," she responded. "I'm not sure he respects his people enough or trusts them enough to give it a real try." With that, we each went on our way.

We didn't have any more collisions, and Gil's solution with the box-maker's off-cuts worked beautifully. Over the next three months we noticed a significant uptick in our orders from Troy's company.

Reflecting on the Chapter

For Supervisors (overseeing front line workers)

- How do your staff react to errors found by customers? Are they perceived as an opportunity, a nuisance, or an interruption?
- Does your company just fix the customer's complaint, or does the complaint result in people improving the processes?
- What were the last errors found by *your* immediate customers (the next operations)? How did you respond to them? Did your boss know about it, and if so, how did they respond to your action?
- What are people in your team used to seeing when there is a mistake? Do they dread mistakes, or do they bring them forward to you? If they bring you the mistakes, are they trying to solve the problem, or trying to blame someone else?

Actions to Take

- The next time you are dealing with a mistake from your team, fix it, and then work with your crew to identify at least five possible causes for the mistake. Ask for each possible cause if it is a FACT, an OPINION, or a GUESS. If it is a fact, what is the data source? See if you can figure out how often that mistake happens for each possible reason.
- From the five possible causes, pick one that you think might also make a difference for other products, and test out some solutions. Track the results. When you find something that works, celebrate with your team (nothing elaborate) and let your boss know what you did and who helped.

For Managers (you have supervisors or managers reporting to you)

Consider all the questions for supervisors for yourself. Then consider the following.

- How does your organization treat quality issues? Really? Are they hidden away, glossed over, ignored or does the company address root causes? What would one of the front-line workers say if you asked and they could be honest?

- If it comes down to making a shipment or meeting quality standards, what is the choice? What does that choice tell your staff? Does that match your company's stated goal?

Actions to Take

- When mistakes or rework are identified and are brought to you for a decision, respond with curiosity about what contributed to the mistake(s). Ask for data about that kind of mistake. What is the history? How often does it happen and when?
- When mistakes or rework are identified, ask your team members for at least five plausible reasons for the problem. For each reason, ask whether it is a FACT, and OPINION, or a GUESS. Ask for the facts and/or reasoning they used to narrow down their selection. Ask them which one they're going to tackle first, and how will they know whether it is working.

Epilogue

At the morning meeting a few weeks after we'd sorted out the problem of the funnels, under the "new stuff" section, Julie commented that over the next month she wanted to sit down with each of us to talk about our own professional development. "I have my ideas, but until I speak with you, they're just my guess. I'd like you to think about three things: what skills you'd like to learn, what parts of the company's operation you'd like to know more about, and what you need to be able to do so your departments run better. Two things that you'd like, and one about what the company needs. Any questions?"

"Is this like a performance evaluation?" asked Peter.

"Not in my mind," responded Julie. "I tell you right away when I think you're doing something that isn't helpful. I've had that conversation with each of you, haven't I?" We looked around the room as we all nodded, each of us remembering when we'd heard from her about something that wasn't up to her standard. "I hope I'm telling you often enough when I think you're doing a good job. I don't think formal performance evaluations are very effective."

"Damn right," growled Peter.

"No. This is so I can help you develop your own skills and grow the way you want to. You're all here because I think you can make a good contribution to the company. But I want you to feel like you're doing things you enjoy and that are rewarding to you."

There were a couple more questions about how it was going to work, and then the conversation moved on, the meeting wrapped up and we all went on our way.

The next day at lunch with Gil and Farah, we were chatting about what it might mean.

"Do you think she'd let us try working in another department?" asked Farah.

"You want my job?" countered Gil.

"No, but you guys know I love shopping. I'm actually really good at it. I think purchasing would be a cool job to have, and I'd love to learn about it. But who would take my job?"

"I'd love to try your job, Farah," I said. I told them about growing up with my dad making things in our shop, and how I loved figuring out how to make stuff.

"Now, at least I know who to ask when I get stuck," Farah observed. "What about you, Gil? What would you like to try?"

"Well, I've been studying accounting at night school." My eyebrows went up; that was news to me. To my mind Gil was the most unlikely accountant – a hard-core outdoors guy, he had been introduced to mountain biking by a school chum, and he now lived to get away into the back country exploring abandoned roads. Not my image of an accountant! "So, I'd love the chance to work with Neil and get some practical exposure to it."

The three of us looked at each other. None of us would have expected that we all had interests in other parts of the company or trying different things. I left the lunch wondering what I would hear if I asked the members of my team about their dreams.

A week later I got a calendar invitation from Julie for lunch. That was unexpected. In the days that followed I learned that she was doing that with every one of us that reported to her. We weren't used to lunch appointments.

"It's so we can be a bit more relaxed," she pointed out, when I asked her about it, once we'd settled in at the restaurant. "If we stayed at the plant both of us would get interrupted."

Over the course of the next 45 minutes we talked about a lot of things, but they all related to my dreams and how I thought I needed to grow, and what the company needed from me.

In summary, I talked about getting more involved in developing new products, and how I wanted to understand more about costs and accounting, and Julie talked about how important it was for me to work on developing my team so I had at least one really strong person that could stand in for me. She also talked about how the whole company – all of us from supervisors to managers and even the crews – needed to learn how to make incremental improvements on a daily basis.

As lunch came to an end, Julie took a sip of her coffee, and sat back. "I want you to know, Trevor, that I'm very pleased with how you've grown over the past 18 months. You've shown that you're interested in learning, that you're interested in your people, and you've changed from a supervisor who was tolerated to a respected leader. It's a big improvement. You can be pleased with what you've accomplished. You have become a good supervisor, and you have the makings of a very good leader."

I sat still. Julie didn't hand out praise lightly. I was slightly amazed, and grateful.

"Thank you," I said quietly. I meant it.

Bathtub Toy Boats

These beautiful bathtub toys were the model for the story in this book. Manufactured from recycled wood (other than the dowels) they stand up to heavy use over years of bathtub time. The colours vary depending on the wood available at the time of manufacture. The boats are weighted so they stay upright, even in fierce bathtub storms. Finished with many coats of marine grade varnish, they are a lasting toy for the special sailor in your family.

Tugboat is approximately 8″ long
Freighter is approximately 13″ long

Order online at www.artiwoodenboats.com.

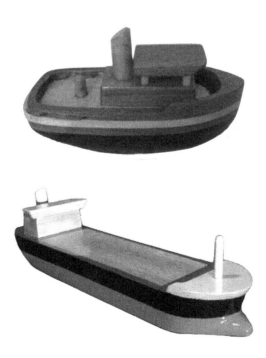

Resources for Supervisors

Books

For individuals who are starting out in a supervisory role, or if the ideas in this book are new to you

Mark Warren. **Job Instruction Sessions Outline**, 2nd Edition. Creative Commons. Tesla², Inc. www.Lulu.com. 2014

Mark has taken the last published Instructor's Guide from the 1946 TWI manual, updated the language, removed the wartime references, and added his own comments and suggestions from his wide experience. It also adds the Reasons column to the Job Instruction Breakdown. Mark is one of the folks who is constantly experimenting with the form of the TWI modules, but because he is so familiar with the history, he remains true to the intent of the original. If you are new to delivering the TWI Job Instruction program, start with this as your guide.

Wally Bock. **Performance Talk—The One-on-One Part of Leadership**

This e-book provides a story-based description of how to have conversations about performance with your staff. Available online only, the story is easy to read and comes with useful workbooks and supporting material. This book is an excellent complement to the TWI Job Relations module because it focuses on the one-to-one interactions of frontline leaders with their team members.

Highly recommended. It is available from www.threestarleadership.com/about-three-star-leadership/working-supervisors-support-kit

Patrick Graupp and Robert J. Wrona. **The TWI Workbook: Essential Skills for Supervisors**, 2nd Ed. New York. Productivity Press. 2015

A solid introduction to the Training Within Industry modules. Some history and discussion of how it works.

The following are recommended after you have some experience in supervisory roles.

Mark Warren and Bryan Lund. **Job Instruction Trainer's Guide**. Creative Commons. Tesla², Inc. www. Lulu.com. 2014

Mark and Bryan have built on their enormous research to produce this manual. It supplements what someone who has gone through Job Instruction has learned, and illustrates how the TWI model has been extended around the world. The authors look at the different levels of instruction, as well as how different agencies addressed the problem of sustaining the use of Job Instruction and the other J programs (JR, JM). They provide a useful section on coaching between sessions and afterwards. This is usually neglected. The other thing this volume provides is a series of checklists and forms that make it easier to present a Job Instruction session. This book is a trainer's guide, not literature. However, it rewards the practitioner with a lot of insight about how to sell and sustain the use of the TWI programs. Well worth the time.

Donald A. Dinero, **The TWI Facilitator's Guide: How to Use the TWI Programs Successfully**. Boca Raton FL, CRC Press: a Productivity Press Book. 2017

This book is geared towards the person who will be instructing the Training Within Industry programs regularly. Dinero provides detailed rationale for many aspects of the TWI programs and directly addresses many of the questions learners will ask. One of his insights is that you should understand why the TWI programs are structured as they are before you tinker with them. This book will help you learn the reasons why TWI works.

Patrick Graupp and Robert Wrona. **Implementing TWI: Creating and Managing a Skills-Based Culture**. New York. Productivity Press. 2010

This book connects Training Within Industry to the concepts of lean and provides case studies that look at examples in manufacturing and health care, among others. There are tools and templates included that you can use to support implementation of TWI in your organization. This will be more helpful for supervisors who have some experience already with their job and the supervisory role.

Jeffrey Liker, Michael Hoseus, and Center for Quality People & Organization. **Toyota Culture: The Heart and Soul of the Toyota Way**. New York. McGraw Hill. 2008

This book focuses on the people-oriented systems Toyota has put in place that instil its founding principles of trust, mutual prosperity, and excellence. It goes over some of Toyota's history and then takes the reader through Toyota's system to attract and develop its people. This will be more helpful for supervisors who have some experience already with their job and the supervisory role.

Web Pages

https://en.wikipedia.org/wiki/Training_Within_Industry

This short summary of Training Within Industry is highly condensed and has some statements that seem to be more editorial than factual. Still, to get started, it's helpful.

All About Lean – www.allaboutlean.com/training-within-industry/

Maintained by Christoph Roser, a Professor at Karlsruhe University of Applied Sciences in Germany this site provides short, easy to read articles about the concepts of lean production. Highly recommended.

The Lean Enterprise Institute – www.lean.org/

The Institute provides seminars and publications. It has one of the most active discussion groups on the web in the whole area of lean thinking. A great resource when you have specific questions.

The TWI Institute – www.twi-institute.com

There are some interesting history pages on the site, as well as details about the programs they provide.

TWI Learning Partnership – www.twilearningpartnership.com

Some helpful and cautionary information about certification for TWI and useful information for the person starting to use the TWI modules.

LinkedIn Supervision Discussion Groups

- Production Supervisor – The Art of Production Management
- Production Supervisor Group
- Operations Managers "Alive"
- TPS Principles and Practice
- TWI – Training Within Industry

These discussion groups offer a lot of insight into the current questions related to supervision. Be aware that people are contributing from their own experience; you should do your own due diligence before accepting what anyone says is the best or only way to do things. Still, with some regular reading, you'll figure out which participants continue to treat the questions posed and the answers offered with curiosity. For me, that is the best mark of a thoughtful contributor.

Lean Frontiers – www.leanfrontiers.com

Lean Frontiers puts on conferences and workshops related to TWI. Their annual TWI Summit is a great place to meet the best in the field and to meet others using the J programs. Lean Frontiers also has some online courses and a number of free webinars that can help you learn about these skills.

Gemba Academy – www.gembaacademy.com

Gemba Academy has a host of free webinars and tutorials about continuous improvement. Within their paid/subscription listings they have almost 100 webinars and tutorials about the TWI J programs. This is a good way to learn the ideas. You still need someone who has done this to coach you through the first few times you use these skills.

Index

Note: Page numbers in italic and bold refer to figures and tables, respectively.

Printed in the United States
by Baker & Taylor Publisher Services